~from~
MILK to MEAT
COMPANION STUDY GUIDE AND WORKBOOK

~*from*~

MILK *to* MEAT

COMPANION STUDY GUIDE AND WORKBOOK

LOREN FINLEY

TATE PUBLISHING
AND ENTERPRISES, LLC

Published by Tate Publishing & Enterprises, LLC
127 E. Trade Center Terrace | Mustang, Oklahoma 73064 USA
1.888.361.9473 | www.tatepublishing.com

Tate Publishing is committed to excellence in the publishing industry. The company reflects the philosophy established by the founders, based on Psalm 68:11,
"The Lord gave the word and great was the company of those who published it."

Book design copyright © 2013 by Tate Publishing, LLC. All rights reserved.
Cover design by Rodrigo Adolfo
Interior design by Jake Muelle

Published in the United States of America

ISBN: 978-1-62746-832-9
1. Religion / Christian Life / Personal Growth
2. Religion / Christian Church / General
13.07.15

AUTHOR'S COMMENTS

All scriptures are Kings James Version (KJV) in this workbook.

The author can be reached in the following ways:

At his Tate author website: lorenfinleymd.tateauthors.com,
At his ministry website: birthrighintl.com,
Or through his author e-mail: lorenfinleyauthor@gmail.com.

Copies of this book can be found in your favorite retail outlets or online, as well as through the author's website.

If you would like to order the book *From Milk to Meat* and/or this workbook, you may do so directly from Tate Publishing through the author's Web site or by contacting Tate Publishing directly. Of course, you can buy them from your favorite bookstores or online sales as you prefer and at your convenience. The workbook was designed for a twelve-session study to accompany the book *From Milk to Meat*.

If you feel this workbook and the book *From Milk to Meat* was a benefit to you, feel free to spread the word to friends, family, and others as well as feel free to discuss it on blogs, forums, or social media. You have permission to use the author's Web site and e-mail above as a reference source for *From Milk to Meat*.

Blessings to you and yours.

TABLES OF CONTENTS

WORKBOOK INTRODUCTION

What is the purpose of this workbook accompaniment to *From Milk to Meat*? It is designed to assist the flock of small to large study groups of *any* association of believers, church, or denomination to understand and receive the *full empowerment* of the Holy Spirit. In time, *From Milk to Meat*, or at least this workbook with the attached *Meat* chapters will be translated into many languages. These truths are universal and need to be widely spread for His body worldwide to use as a teaching tool. This will help believers to be fully empowered and walk in the Holy Spirit with our Lord Jesus.

> And I, brethren, could not speak unto you as unto spiritual, but as unto carnal (*fleshly or self absorbed*), even as unto babes in Christ. I have *fed you with milk, and not with meat*: for hitherto ye were not able to bear it, neither yet now are ye able. For ye are yet carnal: for whereas there is among you envying, and strife, and divisions, are ye not carnal, and walk as men?
>
> 1 Corinthians 3:1–3

> But I fear, lest by any means, as the serpent beguiled Eve through his subtilty (*deception and lies*), so your minds should be corrupted from the *simplicity that is in Christ.*
>
> 2 Corinthians 11:3

This study guide will then assist individuals in those study groups to progress from "milk" to "meat" in their personal and effective spiritual walk with Jesus. The message of the gospel is simple and is not meant to be complex or confusing.

This study guide is to be one of the simple tools the body of Christ can use to teach and empower others to walk in fullness with the Lord. Then those believers can be a truly effective part of the body of Christ, spreading the good news of Jesus in power and truth, to work with the Lord in your gifting to save souls for all time. And then it will be for each of us to receive the ultimate praise at the end of days "Well done, good and faithful servant!" from our Lord Jesus. Your life will be transformed and renewed as you let the Holy Spirit (God) gain control of your being and direct your life for Jesus.

> For when for the time ye ought to be teachers, ye have need that one teach you again which be the first principles of the oracles of God; and are become such as have *need of milk*, and not of strong meat. For every one that *useth milk* is unskilful in the word of righteousness: for he is a *babe*. But

strong meat belongeth to them that are of *full age*, even those who by reason of use have their senses exercised to *discern both good and evil.*

Hebrews 5:12–14

Read this verse over as many times as necessary to set it into your heart. This scripture will be a full teaching in a future book in this book series, but it *is another major reason* for this workbook. It would be easy to spend a whole group session simply discussing this verse, what it means, and what it implies.

As was the Holy Spirit–directed design for *From Milk to Meat*, this workbook will be simple to use and understand. It will help you find and see the mysteries of the word of God as the Holy Spirit (who lives in those belonging to Jesus) reaches into your very soul and teaches and instructs you as to what you need to know.

This twelve-chapter study guide will progress you logically from the basic salvation questions to the final segment of how to have effective prayer in the full power of the Holy Spirit. This is an open-book study, so use *From Milk to Meat* for references and scriptures freely as well as your own Bible and other reference sources. Many answers to questions in the guide are located in the similar named chapters in *From Milk to Meat*. It will be good for you to write answers to questions as it will help you process the answers you consider as you write them down. Also by writing your thoughts, the Lord can speak to you as you write for even more clarifications to questions asked.

There may be some additional scriptures referenced to read and study that will go deeper into the truths being explored that were not included in *From Milk to Meat*. There will also be plenty of opportunity to look up even more scriptures, as the Lord leads, that you feel would be helpful in the discussion or question at hand.

When you are searching for scriptures or words to support what the Lord is leading you to discuss or ponder, there are a few guidelines that are helpful.

- Don't use a single concept or verse to make, create, or confirm any broad thought, doctrinal discussion, or idea.

- Look for when a word is used first in the Bible. That is the most likely and important meaning for that word from God's reverence point.

- Use verses to back up verses to support the concept being discussed.

- If possible, consider the word being evaluated in Hebrew or Greek in its original form and meaning. This is hard if we don't read and speak these languages, but resources (like Strong's) can help.

- Use concepts that are from the Old and New Testament. The Bible is a whole. All scripture is to be used, and it supports itself throughout the Bible. The Old Testament leads to Jesus just as much as the New Testament is about the life and actions of Jesus and the operation of the Holy Spirit released for all people who desire Him. The law covenant of the Old Testament is as relevant to us as the blood (grace) covenant of the New Testament. The entire word of God is God, which is stated in John 1:1.

- Remember that Jesus spoke of love and judgment, not just love and not just judgment. His teachings were balanced. He taught about deliverance and freeing people from bonds and chains (which are the lies of Satan). To be truly free, a person needs the entire story, not just the "easy" parts. You will get that from the word of God and hopefully from this book *From Milk to Meat* and study guide.

- Don't use a verse in isolation, but try to understand the setting the verse was written in. Read up ten verses or more and down ten or more from the verse to see the other parts of the message that are around the verse you are reading. You must bring your Bible to the study groups; you will be searching all around in it during these study sessions. The word of God and our Lord Jesus is the authority, not anything I may have written like this book or study guide.

- You will be asked to write answers to questions. Some of them may seem to be rather blunt or pointed. Some of them may make you uncomfortable. There are no wrong questions or answers, only ones not asked. Once the question and answers are out there, then God, Jesus, the Holy Spirit, you, and the people (maybe) in the group can discuss those questions. This may bring clarity to you and help you see a truth. The next sentence is important for you to understand. Only discuss questions and answers in a group you feel emotionally safe with; be wise and careful with some personal types of questions. This doesn't mean to not share, but just to be wise. It is unfortunate, but not everyone in a group should know all things about you. Some things are between you and Jesus in private, or with a very *small* number of trusted people.

- It may be beneficial to do the study and answer the questions before coming to the group to "do your homework" as they say. Then the time in the group can be spent in great discussion about the truths the Lord is teaching you.

Again, there was no attempt to make *From Milk to Meat* the authoritative reference for any of the chapters or topics written in this book and study guide. That would be completely impossible anyway. God will show you and teach you as the Holy Spirit guides you to other chapters and verses of scripture that compliment what you may be studying at the time. As this series of Milk to Meat books continues, God willing, the topics will get deeper and meatier. But even then, these books are only a resource that is available to *help* you in your walk with Jesus as you make discoveries of truth through the empowerment of the Holy Spirit.

Ultimately, ask Jesus through the gift of the Holy Spirit your questions and give Him the glory for the answers He shows you. It is not for any person to take credit for what God does; that is the opening for spiritual pride, an abomination to the Lord.

What tools can you use to find additional scriptures? There are many actually, and some that I have used personally while writing this book were:

- Online Bible that can be downloaded. Some have word concordances included with them. These are available in many versions; I used King James entirely for this first book, so I used things that had the King James as the base for the computer material.

- Do a word study from any concordance you may have. You will be surprised at how far and wide a single word can take you once you get into this study.

- An unabridged dictionary. This gives a very complete definition of words and helps to clarify meanings of words.

- Strong's Concordance (or others as you find them) was used for King James since that was the version used for this book. Strong's has every word listed, with Hebrew word in Old Testament, and Greek in the New Testament. Some of the words in the King James Version don't spell the *modern* way, so I would use Strong's to make sure I was getting all the versions of a specific word I was looking up.

- Of note, I used no commentaries for information to include in this book or study guide. The purpose was for the word of God and the Holy Spirit as teacher to reveal exactly what He wanted to be written and not to use someone else's interpretations. But these concepts He revealed to me then had to be checked in the Spirit and confirmed with other believers for any errors, which I pray were all caught! This is not to say that commentaries are not to be used in this study process. Of course, they can be very helpful as another tool the Lord may use to help bring clarity to issues. But test those commentaries for truth in the word, of course. This is a big concept, and we will just leave that alone for now. But it could be a great topic to explore as another discussion item as you are getting started in this study?

- Your own memory or marked-up Bible you regularly use. You may have points already highlighted that speak to you as you do this study.

- Ask the Lord to reveal to you a scripture that He wants you to see and read. Just wait on Him and see what He shows you.

Many of the chapters and topics overlap. These chapters can be a stand-alone teaching in many cases; therefore, there are repeated concepts at times among the chapters.

Well, it is time to get started in this study. It is always important to start all things in prayer. Start and end each session you may be doing with this study guide in prayer. Let the Lord lead you in what to pray for at the beginning of the study and what to pray at the end. Prayer is worship of the Lord, and He loves it when we pray so He can answer our prayers.

It is my prayer that the Holy Spirit will guide and teach you as you read and study this workbook guide to *From Milk to Meat*. I pray you will be overfilled and empowered by the Holy Spirit for a full transformation of your life and walk with Jesus. I pray you will discover your gifts from the Lord for use in His body of Christ and for your personal growth spiritually. I pray that you will truly become less of you and more of Him. Amen.

HOW DO I KNOW I'M REALLY SAVED; AND IF I DIE, WILL I GO TO HEAVEN?

Please open in prayer as the Lord leads.

Are you absolutely and completely sure of the answer to the above question? Can you go to your death without fear, knowing without a doubt that you will see Jesus and the Father in heaven and spend eternity with Him? This is probably the most important question that you need to answer in your entire life (From Milk to Meat).

It is a truth that many people who go to church regularly can't answer this question with a positive and confident yes.

So are you sure? Are you really absolutely and completely sure? _____ yes _____no

If you answered yes, how and why are you sure? If you answered no, keep going in this study!

_____

_____

_____

What scriptures helped you to be assured of this? Look them up and record them below.

_____

_____

_____

If you answered no, what is it that is causing you uncertainty? List the reasons that cause you to doubt or to be unsure if you absolutely will go to heaven when you die.

_____

_____

_____

Do you believe that you have a soul that is permanent and created by God?

____Yes ____No

What are some scriptures that support that we have a permanent soul that will be eternal?

_____

_____

_____

_____

Where are the two places that a person's soul will spend eternity in?

1. _____

2. _____

Why are there only two choices as to where our soul goes for all eternity? Do you think there are any other options? _____no _____yes

If you checked yes, where else can a soul go? Do you have any scripture to support this?

_____

_____

_____

What verses in the word do you think are pertinent to the above question of where your soul will go? Here are some words or phrases that may be pertinent to this: holy, holiness, righteousness, judgment of God, grace, and love. Write down some responses here as well as your questions.

_____

_____

_____

_____

Do you have any other unasked questions regarding where your soul goes after death that you would like to discuss?

_____

_____

_____

_____

What do you understand hell to really and truly be? List some of the characteristics of hell as you believe it is.

_____

_____

_____

_____

_____

Why did God create hell? God created everything, even Satan and the fallen angels. What do you think is the purpose of hell?

_____

_____

_____

How does our free will enter into our placement in either heaven or hell?

_____

_____

_____

List some scriptures that relate to the above question.

_____

_____

_____

Do you have other questions about our free will? Why did God give it to us? Do we truly have free will? List anything you may have a question about our free will, so it can be discussed.

_____
_____
_____
_____

Is our free will a gift from God to us? ____yes ____no
Please list verses that may be relevant to this question.

_____
_____
_____

Does our having free will come with consequences for us? What are those consequences?

_____
_____
_____
_____

What is sin? What do you think it really is?

_____
_____
_____

If we sin, what does God think of that? Does it have bad consequences for us?

_____
_____
_____
_____

Look up some scripture as to the result of sin in our life if we don't repent of it.

_____
_____
_____

What do you think *repentance* truly is?

_____

_____

_____

_____

Why did Jesus die on the cross? Do you believe that he lived and died? ____yes ____no

_____

_____

_____

_____

Where is scriptural support that He died for us and what it means for us? Some hints: substitution, innocent sacrifice, lamb of God, love, and free gift from God. This is an important section.

_____

_____

_____

_____

_____

_____

_____

What did Jesus say about His upcoming death on the cross? What did He say it meant? List some scriptures and what they say to you as you read them.

_____

_____

_____

_____

_____

What is the consequence to every person who rejects the free gift of Jesus' death on the cross for us?

_____

_____

_____

_____

Here are facts we need to know and believe about Jesus and the simple things we must do to accept Jesus into our hearts.

In the book is a list of important events that happened 2,000 years ago and what it means for us. Write them down now. (This list is in *From Milk to Meat*.)

1. _____

2. _____

3. _____

4. _____

5. _____

This would be a good time to discuss each of the points one at a time from above. Write down your notes from the discussion.

_____

_____

_____

_____

_____

_____

_____

_____

_____

_____

Do you want to repent now, to truly change your mind and heart, and to turn to God? _____yes

Use the space below to list some of those things you can think of to repent of at this time. Your list will get longer as your walk with Jesus becomes more intimate and you understand truth and love of the Lord more deeply. Praise the Lord.

This is a form of deliverance; it sets you free from your sin and sin's control over your life. Repentance is holy before God. You do not need to share the reasons with the group. God knows and He wants you to share with Him, but you do not need to share with the group, unless you feel it is the proper thing to do and if the Lord leads you to do it. Don't be forced in any way to share anything you feel is not to be shared with a large group.

_____

_____

_____

_____

_____

Do we actually need to ask Jesus to come into our heart? Do we need to say it out loud, to vocalize it? What verses support that? And then what physical act should we do?

_____

_____

_____

What is water baptism? What does it represent spiritually?

_____

_____

_____

_____

Is it really this easy? Is that *all* that is needed? Where is the complexity? State again the only thing we need to do to have eternal life with God in heaven.

_____

_____

_____

Shall we pray to receive Jesus now?

Do you have Jesus in your heart already? _____yes _____no

Do you want to accept Jesus into your heart right now? _____yes _____no

If no, what is holding you back? Be honest, list the real reasons. Jesus loves us more than we can believe, and He wants us all to know Him and receive His free gift of eternal life. There is *nothing* we have to do except receive the free gift of His love.

_____

_____

_____

_____

Is anyone ready right now to accept Jesus into their life if you haven't already? You can say this prayer below out loud, in private or public. I prayed a similar prayer privately at an office desk thirty-four years ago. Or you can call someone or go somewhere and let someone pray it with you. When you do, there will be a party in the heavens for you!

Say this or something like it in your heart and with your lips out loud.

> Dear Lord Jesus, come into my heart. Forgive me of my sins. Wash me and cleanse me. Set me free. Jesus, thank you that you died for me. I believe that you are risen from the dead and that you're coming back again for me. Fill me with the Holy Spirit. Give me a passion for the lost, a hunger for the things of God, and a holy boldness to preach [share] the gospel of Jesus Christ. I'm saved: I'm born again, I'm forgiven, and I'm on my way to heaven because I have Jesus in my heart.
>
> —Revival Ministries International

If you have now, with a sincere heart, prayed this or a similar prayer, we are brothers or sisters with you in earth and in heaven! Praise the Lord! And the heavens have just rejoiced for you!
From Milk to Meat.

You will be excited as you now go through the rest of this study guide along with your personal word of God (bible) and learn the real mysteries of the kingdom of God in earth and heaven. You are going to learn some amazing and exciting things now, and the Holy Spirit will guide and teach you new things that will transform and renew your life.

Now end in prayer as the Lord leads. You can consider the Lord's Prayer if desired.

> Our Father which art in heaven,
> Hallowed be thy name.
> Thy kingdom come.
> Thy will be done in earth, as it is in heaven.
> Give us this day our daily bread.
> And forgive us our debts, as we forgive our debtors.
> And lead us not into temptation, But deliver us from evil:
> For thine is the kingdom, And the power,
> And the glory, for ever.
> Amen.
>
> Matthew 6:9–13

NOW YOU ARE SAVED! WHAT IS NEXT? WHAT DO I DO NOW?

Please open in prayer.

Works versus grace: How does this relate to our love relationship with our Lord?

_____

_____

_____

What do you think *works* means? Think about it first from the Old Testament meaning, then how it still applies today. Try to come to a New Testament definition also, but discuss and understand the Old Testament works of the law.

_____

_____

_____

Old Testament works definition:

_____

_____

_____

_____

_____

New Testament works definition:

_____

_____

_____

_____

Do *works* still apply even though Jesus died for our sins? Jesus died as our sin replacement, so are we subject to the Old Testament covenant of the law or *works*? ____yes ____no

Explain your reasoning or thoughts on this below. The above paragraph is complex. If you take each sentence apart, there is plenty to discuss and learn about.

_____

_____

_____

_____

_____

_____

What scriptures can you list to support your above viewpoint?

_____

_____

_____

_____

Below is a scripture that was one of Paul's explanations of what "works in Christ" really means. Look at these verses in other Bible versions as well, and find other areas in scripture related to this topic. Read above and below this verse to see what other teachings are around it.

> For we are labourers together with God: ye are God's husbandry (*gardeners or workers*), ye are God's building. According to the grace of God which is given unto me, as a *wise masterbuilder*, I have *laid the foundation*, and another buildeth thereon. But let *every man take heed* how he buildeth thereupon. For other *foundation* can no man lay than that is laid, which *is Jesus Christ*. Now if any man *build upon this foundation* gold, silver, precious stones, wood, hay, stubble; *Every man's work shall be made manifest* (*revealed or shown*): for the day shall declare it, because it shall be revealed by fire

(*of the Holy Spirit*); and the fire shall try every man's work of what sort it is. If any man's work abide (*remain*) which he hath built thereupon, he shall receive a reward. If any man's work shall be burned, he shall suffer loss: but he himself shall be saved; yet so as by fire.

1 Corinthians 3:9–15

What does this suggest should be the foundation we build on?

_____

_____

Should we consider carefully how and what we build? Why? What is the difference between gold, silver, and hay or stubble?

_____

_____

_____

_____

_____

What ultimately is the *treasure in heaven* that is the result of the "works" that we do?

_____

_____

Consider if it is the works we do that *we* want to do or the works we do that *God wants us to do*? Is there a difference? Is this related to the difference between gold and stubble or hay? How do we know the difference?

_____

_____

_____

_____

_____

How do our "works" fulfill the great commission to fill heaven with souls? May this be treasure that lasts?

_____

_____

_____

Would you like to end up in heaven with a reward? How does this relate to "build up treasures in heaven" that is in scripture? What are the rewards God will lovingly give us?

_____

_____

_____

_____

Have a discussion about what you think it means that you can be saved "but by fire."

_____

_____

_____

_____

Is there anything we can or need to do that *improves* our ability to receive salvation from God?

_____

_____

What is the *only thing* we need or can do to ensure our salvation?

_____

_____

Now would be a good time to look at another scripture.

> For it is easier for a camel to go through a needle's eye, than for a rich man to enter into the kingdom of God. And they that heard it said, Who then can be saved? And he said, *The things which are impossible with men are possible with God.*
>
> Luke 18:25–27

Read the scripture verses above and below this scripture in your Bible. See if the Lord speaks to you about what this really means as you read these verses. Why did Jesus talk so much in scripture about the danger of riches? This is also part of the "Rich Man" lesson, but now is also a good place to discuss this very important topic. Here is a place for your notes of what you think, and to write down high points of your discussion.

_____

_____

_____

_____

_____

_____

_____

What do you think operating in our freedom of Christ to do whatever we want to do means?

_____

_____

_____

_____

Do you at this time believe that *God does not see our sin* when we belong to Jesus, when Jesus knows us? ____yes____no

So if God doesn't see our sin, are we then allowed to just do whatever we want, even if it is outside the will of God, as we will be forgiven if we *truly* repent? ____yes ____no

Here is some space for notes to discuss the above two questions, and look up some scriptures. Hint: this overlaps a bit with the chapter on "Can We Continue in Sin."

_____

_____

_____

_____

_____

What is the grace of God? Please write below what you think *grace* means? Consider doing a word search on *grace* at this time.

_____

_____

_____

_____

_____

_____

How does faith come into the "grace" concept?

_____

_____

_____

Please list scriptures that show the relationship of faith to grace. Then read them and discuss what they mean to you.

_____

_____

_____

_____

How does "the blood of Jesus" come into relationship to grace?

_____

_____

_____

Would there be any grace if there was no blood of Jesus? His death in obedience to the will of God is the grace that allows us to be cleansed of sins and then presented to the Father clean and without blemish (sin). What do you think of this statement?

_____

_____

_____

_____

_____

Why is this above statement so important?

_____

_____

_____

_____

What does scripture say about boasting about what "we (or I) are doing for God"?

_____

_____

_____

When we do the work of the Lord, who gets the glory?

_____

Why?

_____

Why is it an abomination of God if we try to take God's glory by what *He is having us do*?

_____

_____

_____

What do you think is a good definition of spiritual pride?

_____

_____

What does the word in both Old and New Testament have to say about spiritual pride?

_____

_____

_____

List some scripture here that refers to consequences of spiritual pride.

_____

_____

_____

_____

So now that we live under grace by the love of God because of the death of Jesus, how should we act and live?

_____

_____

_____

_____

List some scriptures that speak to you about how we should act in our love for God now that we are free from death for all eternity.

_____

_____

_____

Is love the driving force in how we should act? _____yes _____no

Explain some of your thinking and reasoning for your answer above, please.

_____

_____

_____

Then one of them, which was a lawyer, asked him a question, tempting him, and saying, Master, which is the great commandment in the law?

Jesus said unto him, Thou shalt *love the Lord* thy God with all thy heart, and with all thy soul, and with all thy mind. This is the *first and great commandment.*

And the *second* is like unto it, Thou shalt *love thy neighbour* as thyself.

On these two commandments hang all the law and the prophets.

Matthew 22:35–40

This is one of the listings of what we commonly call the Great Commandments. What is the first great commandment?

_____

What is the second great commandment?

_____

This would be a good time to discuss the great commandments scripture. Break it into the two parts and all the subparts as well. It is possible to spend the whole time just on this discussion. Why do you think that is? Below will be space for some notes you may want to refer back to over time.

_____

_____

_____

_____

_____

_____

_____

_____

Discuss the first commandment and what it really means for your walk with the Lord. What do you think it means for you? What is the love described here all about?

_____

_____

_____

_____

_____

_____

Love your neighbor as yourself. Why is this such an important commandment from our Lord?

_____

_____

_____

_____

_____

Let us now look at the scriptures referenced in *From Milk to Meat* about love.

> Now the end of the commandment is charity (*Love*) out of a pure heart, and of a good conscience, and of faith unfeigned (*sincere*): From which some having swerved have turned aside unto vain jangling; Desiring to be teachers of the law; understanding neither what they say, nor whereof they affirm.
>
> 1 Timothy 1:5–7

> Owe no man anything, but to love one another: for he that loveth another hath fulfilled the law. For this, Thou shalt not commit adultery, Thou shalt not kill, Thou shalt not steal, Thou shalt not bear false witness, Thou shalt not covet; and if there be any other commandment, it is briefly comprehended in this saying, namely, Thou shalt *love thy neighbour as thyself.* Love worketh no ill to his neighbour: therefore *love is the fulfilling of the law.*
>
> Romans 13:8–10

> For all the law is fulfilled in one word, even in this; Thou shalt love thy neighbour as thyself.
>
> Galatians 5:14

You may want to read up and down from these verses to get more of a picture of context for discussion.

Discuss 1Timothy 1:5–7: What are key points in it?

_____

_____

_____

_____

_____

_____

What are the key points in Romans 13:8–10?

_____

_____

_____

_____

And finally, what are the key points in Galatians 5:14?

_____

_____

_____

_____

Now let us talk about the perfect will of God wrapped in our personal free will.

So how does love relate to our free will to do whatever we want to do?

_____

_____

_____

What should be our guideline for anything (at all) we wish to do?

_____

_____

_____

_____

What scriptures support this thought and action?

_____

_____

_____

_____

_____

Do we need to obey God's commandments? What does that mean to you?

_____

_____

_____

Is it always easy?

_____

_____

_____

_____

Will we have opposition? What form could it take?

_____

_____

_____

_____

Are we still going to have temptations? Are we going to "oops" now and then? What does that mean? What must we do when (not if) we fall down before the Lord (sin), even though we are saved?

_____

_____

_____

Why will there be opposition to our wanting to follow God and love God and our neighbor? Who and what is behind it?

_____

_____

_____

Can we resist these temptations all on our own by our own intellect and thinking? Write down your response to this question.

_____

_____

_____

What does it mean to follow the narrow way and to not take the wide road to destruction (Matthew 7)? What do you think is the narrow way? What do you think is the wide way?

Narrow way:

_____

_____

_____

_____

_____

Wide Way:

_____

_____

_____

_____

Support this above discussion and notes with scripture that speaks to you.

_____

_____

_____

How can we do this?

_____

_____

How do we love God and love our neighbor especially if our neighbor is rotten and mean to us?

_____

_____

_____

Can we do all these things, love our neighbor as ourselves, and love the Lord with all our heart and soul in our *own* power? _____yes _____no.

What are the reasons for your answer?

_____

_____

Do you have scriptures to support this view?

_____

_____

_____

Did God give us a helper? To put it in plain terms, did God provide a tool for us that we can engage (or he engages us) to do the perfect will of God? _____yes _____no

And the name of that comforter, helper, teacher, and guide is? _____

And what is the character of the Holy Spirit? What is a key verse that explains exactly who the Holy Spirit really is?

_____

_____

_____

For there are three that bear record in heaven, the Father, the Word, and the Holy Ghost; and *these three are one.*

1 John 5:7

Here is space for notes for further discussion that may arise in general about this chapter.

_____

_____

_____

_____

_____

_____

_____

_____

CHARACTERISTICS AND MANIFESTATIONS OF THE HOLY SPIRIT

Please open in prayer.

As presented in the book *From Milk to Meat*, this chapter is mostly a listing of characteristics of the Father, Son, and Holy Spirit, with some author interpretations thrown in. Please take the time to consider and add to the lists of characteristics of the Father, Son, and Holy Spirit. The list, when complete, will be very long for each of them.

What do you think of when you think of God? What is He really like? What does He mean to you personally?

_____

_____

_____

_____

_____

_____

_____

What scriptures have most spoken to you about the characteristics of God?

_____

_____

_____

_____

_____

_____

What does the phrase, "The sovereignty of God," mean to you?

_____

_____

_____

Do you have some scriptures to list here related to God's sovereignty?

_____

_____

_____

What does "The righteousness of God" mean to you?

_____

_____

_____

_____

And what are some scriptures that relate or clarify what *righteousness* means?

_____

_____

_____

And now for the really hard one: what does "fear of the Lord" mean to you?

_____

_____

_____

_____

_____

_____

_____

The *fear of the Lord tendeth to life*: and he that hath it shall abide satisfied; he shall not be visited with evil.

Proverbs 19: 23

Consider this proverb. Study it deeply. Find other scriptures that relate to "fear of the Lord," there are many. Why did the Lord in His scripture discuss "fear of the Lord" so often if it wasn't incredibly important! God gives us rules to live by, and if we do, we are blessed, and if we don't, we are not blessed (or cursed).

This is as relevant now, as in ancient days. If we live in awe and love of the Father, Son, and Holy Spirit, we will obey His commandments and be blessed. What happens if we don't obey? This may be a difficult discussion, but it is important to your understanding of the kingdom of God.

_____

_____

_____

_____

_____

_____

_____

_____

Do you have some favorite scriptures you want to reference that speak to you about the fear of the Lord, the reverent awe and majesty of our God? Also, do you have a verse that is of the "fire and brimstone" type of fear of the Lord you wish to list and discuss? Now have a great discussion.

_____

_____

_____

_____

_____

Discussion notes in review about the characteristics of God and fear of the Lord.

_____

_____

_____

_____

_____

_____

_____

What do you think are the characteristics of Jesus? What is Jesus all about? What was the purpose for His ministry? This is a long list!

_____

_____

_____

_____

_____

_____

_____

_____

_____

_____

_____

What scripture verses back up what you listed as key things that make up what Jesus means to you?

_____

_____

_____

_____

_____

_____

_____

_____

Why do we need to learn about the Holy Spirit and the gifts of the Holy Spirit?

_____

_____

_____

_____

Now concerning spiritual gifts, brethren, I would not have you ignorant.

1 Corinthians 12:1

But the manifestation of the Spirit is given to every man to profit withal (*everyone*).

1 Corinthians 12:7

Did these two verses help you answer the above question? Read all of 1 Corinthians 12, it is a major source of information about the gifts and manifestations of the Holy Spirit. What leapt out at you as you read chapter 12?

_____

_____

_____

_____

_____

Who is the Holy Spirit? What are the characteristics and operations of the Holy Spirit? There is space for your notes below. This is important to the reason you are present in this study! You are here to learn about the Holy Spirit and how He will transform and renew your life!

_____

_____

_____

_____

_____

_____

_____

_____

_____

_____

_____

Please write scriptures that back up the main points of your discussion from above about the Holy Spirit.

_____

_____

_____

_____

_____

_____

Now we will look at the manifestations of the Holy Spirit.

Have you ever been told that the "gifts" and "time of miracles" were present during the time of Jesus, but they aren't manifest now? _____yes _____no

Do you believe these gifts truly are available to believers now? _____yes _____no

If you answered no, then you are at the right place by participating in this study. It is my prayer you will come to the truth that the gifts of the Holy Spirit are here now, active, and available to every believer!

> *The gifts of the Holy Spirit are as alive today as they were in the early church two thousand years ago. These gifts are every bit as available to believers today as they ever have been. It is a lie of Satan if anyone says these gifts are not active in believers today!*
>
> *—From Milk to Meat*

In fact, to attempt to deny the operation of the gifts of the Holy Spirit is and has been a *major scheme* of Satan to confuse, deceive, and destroy the church. In another teaching in an upcoming book, we will go into this in depth.

Notes for discussion from the above:

_____

_____

_____

_____

_____

_____

Below is the list of nine gifts of the Holy Spirit. For this study, record what you feel are the truths and effects of each of these gifts. Use *From Milk to Meat*, your Bible, and other sources you want to fill in these notes.

1. *Word of wisdom.* Notes:

    _____

    _____

    _____

2. *Word of knowledge.* Notes:

    _____

    _____

    _____

    _____

    _____

3. *Faith.* Notes:

    _____

    _____

    _____

    _____

    _____

4. *Gifts of healing.* Notes:

    _____

    _____

    _____

    _____

    _____

5. *Working of miracles.* Notes:

    _____

    _____

    _____

    _____

    _____

6. *Prophecy.* Notes:

_____

_____

_____

_____

_____

7. *Discerning of spirits.* Notes:

_____

_____

_____

_____

_____

8. *Diverse (different) kinds of tongues.* The gift of tongues is actually in two parts. Please note: this is the author's viewpoint and is supported by scripture and further explained as a separate chapter in this workbook.

- *The first is your personal prayer language.*
- *The second form of tongues is meant to be spoken to the body of Christ, which needs to be interpreted. This gift is related to the prophetic gift. This gift may or may not be the same as your personal prayer language.*

—*From Milk to Meat*

Notes:

_____

_____

_____

_____

_____

_____

_____

_____

_____

_____

9. *Interpretation of tongues.* Notes:

_____

_____

_____

_____

_____

_____

_____

_____

_____

This was a summary of the nine gifts listed in scripture. They interact together in amazing and powerful ways. They are meant for the training and empowerment of His body of believers to do the work of the Lord for His glory. If you are in need of more information on gifts of the Spirit, there are many fine books on the Holy Spirit available that go deeper. These gifts of the Spirit are real and effective today, and I have seen them in operation all around me.

—From Milk to Meat

But all these worketh that one and the selfsame Spirit, dividing to every man severally as he will. For as the body is one, and hath many members, and all the members of that one body, being many, are one body: so also is Christ....*But now hath God set the members* every one of them in the body, *as it hath pleased him.* And if they were all one member, where were the body? *But now are they many members, yet but one body.* And the eye cannot say unto the hand, I have no need of thee: nor again the head to the feet, I have no need of you.

1 Corinthians 12:11–12, 18–21

Please list some scriptures that spoke to you during this exercise and writing of the characteristics and manifestations of the nine gifts of the Holy Spirit.

_____

_____

_____

_____

_____

_____

_____

_____

For the final section of this study, how have you personally seen the gifts in operation in your life or the life of your body of believers? As you feel led by the Lord, share this with the group.

Notes:

_____

_____

_____

_____

_____

Now we are getting deeper into His truths. And they will set you free!

EMPOWERMENT BY THE HOLY SPIRIT

Please open in prayer.

What does the term *empowerment* mean to you?

_____

_____

_____

_____

How do we see the Holy Spirit in action?

_____

_____

_____

_____

What scriptures support your above thoughts?

_____

_____

_____

_____

What do the terms *wind* and *breathe* mean to you in relation to the Holy Spirit?

_____

_____

_____

_____

_____

_____

What scriptures come to mind when you think of wind or breath of God?

_____

_____

_____

_____

_____

What does scripture say about giving the glory to God?

_____

_____

_____

_____

What scripture supports the above?

_____

_____

_____

_____

When you hear the phrase, "Give place to the Holy Spirit in your life," what does that say to you?

_____

_____

_____

_____

What scriptures support your thoughts from the above question?

_____

_____

_____

What do you think "grieving and quenching the Holy Spirit" is all about? How does that happen? What are the consequences to a believer that grieves the Spirit of God?

_____

_____

_____

_____

_____

_____

_____

_____

What scriptures should you place here that relate to the above question? This is important.

_____

_____

_____

_____

What does the phrase, "Pick up your cross daily and follow me," mean to you?

_____

_____

_____

_____

_____

How do we really do this? How can we do this?

_____

_____

_____

_____

_____

How does God reveal his secrets and mysteries to us?

_____

_____

_____

_____

Support this with scripture that speaks to you.

_____

_____

_____

_____

When you read the Bible, the word of God, how exciting is it to you? Is it dry and boring and hard to get through at times? _____yes_____no.

If you answered yes, why do you think it is boring or difficult to read?

Author's note: I thought it was dry and boring for up to twenty years! I didn't seem to get anything out of it. Even though I was a believer (although very carnal, ouch), it was hard for me to read the Bible. And it didn't make any difference which version I used either. As I said in *From Milk to Meat*, it had been close to ten years that I hadn't even opened my bible before God really touched me. No wonder my life was a *mess*!

Notes for your answer and discussion:

_____

_____

_____

_____

Do you know or understand the power that enables you to make the word of God come alive for you when you read it? What is the power that reveals the mysteries of God in the word?

_____

_____

Please write and discuss the scripture that relates to the above. Can you find other scriptures than the ones listed in *From Milk to Meat*? Take some time to discuss these scriptures and what they mean. Scriptures:

_____

_____

_____

_____

Discussion notes:

_____

_____

_____

_____

_____

_____

How do we get more faith? How do we believe even more what we can't actually see, feel, or touch?

_____

_____

_____

_____

Do you want to be free of fear? Fear of man, fear of circumstances, and free of worldly concerns? How does this happen? How do we truly remove all the fears that surround and sometimes paralyze us?

_____

_____

_____

_____

What scriptures support how you can become fearless? How about in the Old Testament?

_____

_____

_____

_____

What will be the effects in your life when you are empowered by the Holy Spirit?

_____

_____

_____

_____

What scriptures can you find to support this?

_____

_____

_____

What does "Becoming a child of God," "an heir of the kingdom," and "rights and privileges of a Son of the King" mean to you?

_____

_____

_____

_____

_____

_____

Please record scripture to support what this means to you.

_____

_____

_____

Do you believe we have the power to do what Jesus did while He was on earth? ___yes____no

Record your thoughts on this and the scriptures that relate to your reasoning.

_____

_____

_____

_____

_____

_____

What do we have to have and do to have this power? Support it with scripture.

_____

_____

_____

_____

_____

Get ready for the next chapter!

ASK AND RECEIVE THE HOLY SPIRIT

Please open this session in prayer

Now we are fully into the really good stuff relating to the Holy Spirit and have arrived at a decision point. We've been describing characteristics, manifestations, and empowerment by the Holy Spirit, but now what? What good does it do to just understand these truths with your mind and not have it be a part of your life?

—From Milk to Meat

Are you ready at this time to ask the Holy Spirit to reside in you, guide you, and teach you directly? _____yes _____no.

If you answered yes, then you can pray and ask for the Holy Spirit *to fully* come into you now! At the end of this section is a prayer you could use as a framework and ask the Holy Spirit to come fully into you.

If you answered no, then continue with this study please. This is the whole reason you are here; to learn these truths about the Holy Spirit and come to the decision regarding receiving gifts from the Lord, including the Holy Spirit in full power and authority! Below is space to record any questions or concerns you may still have or areas you desire more clarity about.

_____

_____

_____

_____

_____

_____

_____

_____

Do you understand that once you ask the Holy Spirit fully into you, that you have God Himself (Holy Spirit) residing in you, which makes you a temple of God? As a believer you have *a measure of the Holy* Spirit when you asked Jesus into your heart. This next step of asking is for more, the full meal deal, the empowerment and *fire baptism* by the Holy Spirit of God.

The above agrees with the author's personal experience as well. Once I truly *asked* for God (the Holy Spirit) to *fully come in and overfill me*, I was immediately and radically changed. But I had known the Lord for the prior thirty-two years, but was missing *this piece*!

Here is a *key* to the entire reason for this book and workbook. My goal in these writings is to show how to get that *extra charge* of the holy Spirit. This is needed so that God through the Holy Spirit can guide and help us to do the will of God as we release to Him the *control* of our self to do exactly that. This section could take an entire book to fully explore.

Is this walking the "narrow way" with Jesus? The following sections will address more of these types of questions.

If this is not clear to you, write down the thoughts that you need clarified about being the temple of God, or that God lives in you as a believer. Then ask the Holy Spirit to help you to receive the clarification you need.

_____

_____

_____

_____

_____

_____

_____

_____

Below is a scripture from Jesus when he spoke and taught about asking.

> And I say unto you, *Ask*, and it shall be given you; *seek*, and ye shall find; *knock*, and it shall be opened unto you. *For every one that asketh receiveth*; and he that seeketh findeth; and to him that knocketh it shall be *opened*. If a son shall ask bread of any of you that is a father, will he give him a stone? or if he ask a fish, will he for a fish give him a serpent? Or if he shall ask an egg, will he offer him a scorpion? If ye then, being evil, know how to give good gifts unto your children: how much more shall your heavenly Father *give the Holy Spirit to them that ask him*.
>
> Luke 11:9–13

What did this scripture say to you about asking for the Holy Spirit? Reread it if needed and really consider what the truth is here.

_____

_____

_____

_____

_____

Look up and consider scriptures and discuss how we are able to come to Jesus? What is the power that enables that? If you know Jesus, what led you to him?

_____

_____

_____

_____

Can receiving the full empowerment of the Holy Spirit simultaneously occur at the salvation experience, or is this required to be asked for separately? Look up references and consider this. What is the general method God uses? (Author's opinion from the word is whatever God wants to do will occur)! It is important at this time to see and read the scriptures that talk about this specifically. Acts is a good book for many of these verses.

Scriptures:

_____

_____

_____

_____

_____

Discussion notes:

_____

_____

_____

_____

_____

_____

_____

This would be a good place for discussion and notes about your thoughts as you read in *From Milk to Meat* in various places about having a "touch of the Holy Spirit" and are "saved but as through fire." Another point to discuss would be how asking and then receiving an overfilling of the Holy Spirit (and all that means) relates to the wise and unwise virgins in the ten virgins parable? Does this relate to needing to take another step to get the *full empowerment* of the Holy Spirit, by the fact that we *usually (rarely, God just does it)* have to specifically *ask* for the Holy Spirit? What happens if you don't take this step? What scriptures are used to support this discussion? Could this be related to the *fire* of the Holy Spirit Jesus baptizes with? These are in-depth questions.

_____

_____

_____

_____

_____

_____

_____

_____

_____

_____

_____

_____

_____

How does the Holy Spirit have a relationship to the work you do for the Lord in love? What lasting fruit will occur if it is *you* doing the work and not God *directing* your work? Is it somehow related to doing things from your flesh or mind or doing things from God/heart/Holy Spirit directed?

_____

_____

_____

_____

_____

_____

_____

_____

Ask yourself: are you doing what you want from your own mind, intellect, and personal wants and asking God to bless it? Are you *only* doing exactly what is the perfect will of God for you to do? How do you *know* the difference? How are you *sure* of the difference? Are you following the narrow path or the wide path to the ditch? How do we see the narrow path so we are able to not stray from it?

_____

_____

_____

_____

_____

So what happens when we ask for the overfilling of the Holy Spirit? God is allowed complete and absolute control of all you are or will become. It is the "fire" of the Holy Spirit that comes from Jesus. It is our release of control of our self (mind or intellect) over our actions and letting God and Jesus (through the Holy Spirit) control and truly guide our lives. And it is a whole lot of fun when God is in control! You will have true freedom to really live then! The chains holding you down in fear will be broken!

—*From Milk to Meat*

What do you think of the concept of *overfilling* of the Holy Spirit versus *filled* (implying a one-time or completed act)? Consider how the Lord talks about rivers, streams, drink, drinking, flowing, pours, etc. Put down your thoughts and support it with scripture about the need for filling and refilling of the Holy Spirit of God! Why do we need a constant refilling of the Holy Spirit (Hint: to give away, don't you need to refill)?

Scriptures to help understand this:

_____

_____

_____

_____

_____

Discussion notes:

_____

_____

_____

_____

_____

_____

_____

Let us now look at some scriptures used in *From Milk to Meat.* They speak to the above questions.

Blessed are they which do hunger and thirst after righteousness: for they shall be filled (*with the Holy Spirit*).

Matthew 5:6

Jesus answered and said unto her, "Whosoever drinketh of this water shall thirst again: But whosoever drinketh of the water that I shall give him shall never thirst; but the water that I shall give him shall be in him a well of water springing up into everlasting life."

John 4:13–14

In the last day, that great day of the feast, Jesus stood and cried, saying, "If any man thirst, let him come unto me, and drink. He that believeth on me, as the scripture hath said, out of his belly shall flow rivers of living water. (*But this spake he of the Spirit, which they that believe on him should receive: for the Holy Ghost was not yet given; because that Jesus was not yet glorified [risen to heaven]*)."

John 7:37–39

Discussion notes for these three scriptures:

_____

_____

_____

_____

_____

_____

_____

Read the parable of the ten virgins in Matthew 25:1–13.

What do you think of the teaching about how the Holy Spirit relates to the ten virgins parable? Read the related section in *From Milk to Meat*, and record your discussion notes below.

_____

_____

_____

_____

_____

_____

_____

What would be your definition of carnal Christians? What scriptures did you use to support this?

_____

_____

_____

_____

_____

_____

Read the parable of the wide and narrow gate from Matthew 7:13–14. In what way did this speak to you?

_____

_____

_____

_____

_____

What is the straight gate? Who is it that passes through this gate? Are these people believers and have a choice of two paths to go down?

_____

_____

_____

_____

What is the wide way?

_____

_____

_____

_____

_____

What is the narrow way?

_____

_____

_____

_____

_____

What is the end result of following the narrow way?

_____

_____

What is the end result of following the wide way?

_____

_____

How does this all relate to dying to self daily, pick up your cross daily, and follow Jesus? What could be some key words or concepts here?

_____

_____

_____

_____

_____

_____

Look up and discuss where Jesus talked about that it wasn't enough to just say *you* know Jesus, but Jesus needs to know you. What does Jesus require?

_____

_____

_____

_____

_____

_____

The Lord is not allowing me to sugar coat these truths and avoid controversy; He wants the real truth based on His Word (which is Jesus) out there for His Body to see and understand and is using me in some small part for His message. The Lord wants this information available so we can all participate in His great commission of saving lost souls using the full resources of God available to us.

What an awful thing it will be if we realize at the end of days that we were the cause of somebody not going to heaven for all eternity because we said "no" to a request of the Lord.

—From Milk to Meat

Loren Finley

Discussion notes from the above section:

_____

_____

_____

_____

_____

_____

_____

What scripture is commonly called "the Great Commission"?

_____

So what does Jesus say we should do about sharing what we know about the truths of the Gospel?

_____

_____

_____

_____

_____

Discuss the phrase that is very commonly stated or thought by many people today: "They are adults. Don't push them. It is up to them to decide about God or not." Have you ever heard this or thought it yourself?

_____

_____

_____

_____

_____

So what is really being said by this phrase? I will offer an opinion in straight truth. Are we to just quietly let our friends and family not know about Jesus and all it means, and then they may be eternally separated from God for all time in hell? Really? Aren't we to contend for our faith? Aren't we to do battle for God? Why? (Now this doesn't mean to go crazy, but to seek the Lord and do what *He asks*. And it may be simple, little things, relationship building in love with gentle words over coffee, etc.). So what would this look like for you in your life?

_____

_____

_____

_____

_____

_____

_____

_____

And what is the power that will give us the strength, guidance, energy, lack of fear, or embarrassment to do what God wants us to do? And isn't this what God wants us to do, to help bring all the lost souls to Him that will? What is more important in this life than that? And God will not ask you to do more than you are capable of doing; when He asks you to do something, you are ready and have all the resources you need in hand (by and through the Holy Spirit).

_____

_____

_____

_____

_____

Decision time!

So it is now crunch time! Do you want to have the full power of God Himself living in you? Do you want to have God directly guiding you in all things? Do you want to have the true peace that you can only get when you have God residing in you? Do you truly desire to be one of those going down the narrow path with Jesus hand in hand?

Then just ask Him to truly come into your heart right now! Ask Him to fill you to overflowing with the Holy Spirit and for Him to come to you, teach you, and guide you! Ask Him to come with such a degree you are just plain overfilled, and the Holy Spirit will now just ooze out and all around you for His will! Ask to be one of His lights for the world. Ask and pray this above with true sincerity, and He will come to you! Then you will have true joy of the Lord and a peace you can never believe regardless of your circumstances.

—From Milk to Meat

Jesus answered and said unto him, If a man love me, he will *keep my words*: and my Father will love him, and *we will come unto him*, and *make our abode (live in you) with him.*

John 14:23

Are you ready now? _____yes.

If not, what is holding you back?

_____

_____

_____

_____

In *From Milk to Meat,* I mentioned some guidelines about spiritual warfare, spiritual transfer, and praying in the name and blood of Jesus. This would be a good place to discuss your thought on that section.

_____

_____

_____

_____

_____

_____

_____

_____

_____

Now, if you want to ask for more of the Holy Spirit, don't wait. Do it now. You can do this privately between you and Jesus, or individually with experienced believers, or even as part of a group prayer, with each individual in sincere and complete repentance, forgiveness, and agreement with this desire. All you have to do is Ask Him.

My prayer is that as you read, study, and meditate on this, you will ask for the Holy Spirit from God to overfill you and set you free! Ask the Holy Spirit to come into your heart and take control of all of you. My prayer is you are now overfilled with the Spirit and just can't wait to discover His perfect will for you and how exciting that will be for you!

If you wish to pray a prayer to overfill with the Holy Spirit, what is listed below would be a good guideline for the prayer.

"Jesus, I ask in your name and covered by your blood to overfill me with the Holy Spirit. Come into my heart to such a degree that the Holy Spirit just oozes out of me for all to see. I praise you Father, and thank you Jesus for your gift of the Holy Spirit to guide, teach and comfort me. Fill me with your fire of the Holy Spirit for your glory. I praise you for the gifts of the Spirit that you have given me from the day of creation. Please empower me by those gifts and your Holy Spirit to be a part of your Body of Christ and to further your Gospel of Grace and Salvation to all those who don't yet know. Guide and protect me from Satan and all the evil spirits loose in the world by the power of the Spirit and your holy angels, and keep these evil spirits under the feet of Jesus from His throne in heaven. I praise you Father for your gift of the Holy Spirit and how He will open up the Word of God and the mysteries of your Kingdom to me now. Amen."

—*From Milk to Meat*

Wow! If you prayed this or a similar prayer, you have received the power of the living God in you. Thank Him and praise Him. He gets the glory for this wonderful event. And nothing pleases Him more than seeing His children getting more of His gifts! And now, you get to go on in the learning process for the full empowerment of your walk with Jesus.

Praise the Lord!

_____

_____

_____

_____

_____

_____

_____

_____

_____

_____

_____

_____

GOD HAS NOT CHANGED

Please open this session in prayer.

This may be a hard session emotionally for many as it addresses directly some very serious topics.

God has not changed from the beginning of time, and He won't before the end of time either. What does this mean for us? Why is this relevant for us today and at this time?

—*From Milk to Meat*

What do you think about this statement?

_____

_____

_____

_____

_____

_____

How do you think it might relate to our freedom of choice to choose Christ (or not)? What did Christ do for us that allow God the Father to not have to judge our sin?

_____

_____

_____

_____

_____

Please read and then discuss the verse below.

Nevertheless I tell you the truth; It is expedient for you that I go away: for if I go not away, the Comforter will not come unto you; *but if I depart, I will send him unto you.*
And when he is come, *he will reprove (convict) the world of sin, and of righteousness, and of judgment:* Of sin, because they believe not on me; Of righteousness, because I go to my Father, and ye see me no more; Of judgment, because the prince of this world (*Satan*) is judged.

John 16:7–11

_____

_____

_____

_____

_____

_____

Is there an Old Testament God and a New Testament God? This is not a silly question, as some people may truly think this is true, that He changed somehow after the death of Jesus. What do you think and why? Has God changed? If you think He has, why do you feel this way? Do you have any scripture to support this viewpoint?

_____

_____

_____

_____

_____

Discuss the statement below made in *From Milk to Meat.*

There is only one God, one Jesus, and one Holy Spirit. God loves us more than we can imagine or believe. He loved us so much He sent His beloved Son, Jesus, to die a horrible death on the cross so He could remain exactly who He is and still make a way for us to get in a position to be able to commune with God the Father for all time. This is the only way we could have been allowed to live in heaven with God and Jesus; while at the same time maintaining His righteousness and holiness to punish sin.

Write below the notes from your thoughts and discussion of this paragraph. There is a lot of meat and important concepts in these brief sentences about the holiness and righteousness of God.

_____

_____

_____

_____

_____

_____

_____

_____

_____

_____

_____

Was this an act of deep and unbelievable love from God the Father to send Jesus, the Son of God, His only begotten Son, to die for us? Would we as humans send our only earthly child to real torture and death for people that were horrible to us to begin with?

_____

_____

_____

_____

_____

Did the holiness of God change after He sent Jesus to die, or does it just fully reveal His love?

_____

_____

How does this relate to our freedom to make personal choices? In particular, the ultimate personal choice of whether to believe Jesus is the Son of God and then to follow Him.

_____

_____

_____

_____

Would we be able to give so much love and free choice to our own earthly children when they became accountable for their own actions that they could *choose* to live absolutely and completely separate from us? And we had done nothing wrong, only loved them to the depths of our heart? And once they made that decision, they would permanently and without ability to "change their minds" now be *unable* to *ever* make contact with us in any manner for the rest of our life? Forever and permanent without recourse! How would we feel?

_____

_____

_____

_____

_____

_____

How do you think God and Jesus feel when His children reject His free gift of love that leads to their eternal life with Him, especially as He loves us all so much and gave so much in sacrifice to make this possible for us?

_____

_____

_____

_____

_____

What is the penalty that God *has to* impose for those who do reject His Son?

_____

_____

Do you see how God can be so full of love and at the same time remain and be completely holy and righteous? How He can love the sinner, but hate sin?

_____

_____

_____

_____

_____

So what is the plan God made from the beginning of time to give us all an "escape clause" from eternal death? That we are sinners and not be judged and condemned? That we can commune with Him for all time in heaven, even though *we don't deserve it?*

_____

_____

_____

_____

_____

_____

_____

What do you think about the phrase: We must listen, hear, and then obey the Lord our God? What happens if we don't?

_____

_____

_____

_____

_____

_____

_____

Now will be included some scriptures relating to what Jesus will do at the end of days for every person. This is called the Judgment of God. Jesus talked about this; we better teach about it as well so people understand this truth.

And it is *very simple*; Jesus will screen you after you die and see if He knows you. How does He know you?

_____

_____

_____

If Jesus does know you by the Spirit, then He can present you clean of sin to the Father, so God doesn't then have to condemn you for all time by placing you in hell. It is simply an evaluation of your actions and decisions in this life related to "yes" or "no" about believing and living for Jesus, and then just like a court on this planet, you are either innocent or guilty and are placed in one of two places. That is it. *It is that simple*, but that *serious* as well. God wants all to be saved who will, but they *must* want it and then *obey*.

> And I saw heaven opened, and behold a white horse; and he [*Jesus*] that sat upon him was called Faithful and True, and in righteousness he doth *judge* and make war.
>
> Revelation 19:11

> And whosoever was not found written in the *book of life* was cast into the lake of fire.
>
> Revelation 20:15

> My sheep hear my voice, and I know them, and they follow me: And I give unto them eternal life; and they *shall never perish*, neither shall any man pluck them out of my hand. My Father, which gave them me, is greater than all; and no man is able to pluck them out of my Father's hand.
>
> John 10:27–29

> But after thy hardness and impenitent heart treasurest up unto thyself wrath against the day of wrath and revelation of the righteous judgment of God; Who will *render to every man according to his deeds*....For there is no respect of persons with God. For as many as have sinned without law shall also perish without law: and as many as have *sinned in the law shall be judged by the law*.
>
> Romans 2:5–6, 11–12

Discussion notes:

_____

_____

_____

_____

_____

_____

_____

_____

_____

_____

If Jesus knows you, you will go to heaven. Does He really know you? Are you absolutely sure? If not, please reread that chapter in this book immediately!

—*From Milk to Meat*

_____

_____

_____

_____

_____

In *From Milk to Meat,* some comments were made to help explain some of the above concepts.

What did you think about the *Garden of Eden* discussion?

_____

_____

_____

_____

_____

The *Covenant of the Law*: what does this mean to you?

_____

_____

_____

_____

_____

_____

What is the *Blood Covenant of Jesus*, sometimes called the Grace Covenant? Discuss your thoughts on this. Why is blood needed? What is so important about the blood of Jesus?

_____

_____

_____

_____

_____

_____

_____

_____

Discuss your thoughts on the fact the Jesus is Lord and the earth is His footstool. Where does this place Satan?

_____

_____

_____

_____

_____

_____

Now we get to another very important part of this teaching. And it is likely to make people squirm or to become upset. But the Lord is requiring this to be included now.

If Jesus knows you, this is review regarding your salvation. But there is much *beyond* our salvation experience that we need to understand about the Kingdom of God.

Consider this discussion as it relates to family and friends of yours who do *not* know the Lord *yet* and how important it is for *them* to know Him! What if *you* were the only one that God was able to send to them to help them see this and you *didn't obey and go*? Do you see how this must occur even if it is hard and difficult for you personally, if God sends you?

Here is place for some discussion notes about the preceding paragraphs.

_____

_____

_____

_____

_____

Jesus is the only way to God.

He is the gateway, the only door to eternal life in heaven.

This statement above will become offensive to people who reject the free gift of God and will increasingly cause serious persecution for believers everywhere. Persecution coming is in the scriptures from Old to New Testament, from Genesis to Revelation. Do we know when this may come? Absolutely not, but it could be soon. And to say, "Jesus is the only way," even in your own home, may become a hate crime in the near future. Will you "go along and stay silent" or fearlessly speak the truth in love anyway? Are you ready to be arrested for your faith in Jesus? People right now, today, in some parts of the world, are being murdered for professing Jesus! Is it possible we may be near or at the early stages of the end times of the bible?

Are you ready for this if it really comes to this level of persecution? It is your eternal soul and placement in heaven or hell that is truly at stake. This is *serious*. But it should not cause fear but rejoicing because persecution must come before Jesus can return to rule and reign again. This is very clear in scripture, both in the Old and New Testament. Everyone needs to know exactly the truth and what the cost could truly become. It wasn't a game in the past; why do we think it might not be just as serious in the future and for us personally? Doesn't Jesus say to "watch" and "be ready"?

_____

_____

_____

_____

_____

_____

_____

_____

_____

_____

_____

_____

_____

_____

_____

Jesus is the only way to the Father! His blood is the only way to the Father, and we have to believe, repent, and be transformed by the Holy Spirit.

*And we get to make that choice, yes or no about believing in Jesus. And the eternal consequences that attach to it are completely clear. One place or the other; heaven or hell.

*God had a plan to help and save us and not change or diminish His holiness at the same time!

—From Milk to Meat

For God so loved the world, that he gave his only begotten Son, that whosoever believeth in him should not perish, but have *everlasting life*

John 3:16

Notes:

_____

_____

_____

_____

_____

In summary, God loves us so much He made a way for us to spend eternity with Him, even though we don't deserve it. We have to believe and walk with Jesus to arrive, however. If Jesus doesn't know you, He can't present you to the Father. And in the ultimate expression of God's love, and even though it pains Him greatly to lose anyone, the Father in heaven truly will let each person make their own choice as to whether they will accept the free gift of God's love. And then each person will be awarded exactly the reward or placement to heaven or hell as a result of their personal free will choices.

—From Milk to Meat

It is now time to talk again about hell or eternal separation from God. Hell is a horrible place! What are some scriptures that describe hell? Did Jesus talk much about hell in the Gospels and Revelation? And if Jesus clearly did, shouldn't we understand what hell really is?

_____

_____

_____

_____

_____

How would you describe hell? Support it from scripture, not feelings.

_____

_____

_____

_____

_____

Do you know anyone who does not know the Lord, but is a *good person*? Where do you think they will go if they don't hear, believe, and then act on the saving love of Jesus? Do you want this person to go to hell for all time? Would you be willing to put yourself out to share the good news of Jesus so they know and can then make an informed decision for their very souls?

_____

_____

_____

_____

_____

Is there anything more important in this life than helping every loved one or friend we know to learn the truth about Jesus, and what it means?

_____

_____

_____

_____

_____

_____

_____

_____

After that, what about people that we don't know, but they haven't received the good news?

_____

_____

_____

_____

Space for final notes or discussion thoughts:

_____

_____

_____

_____

_____

CONTINUE IN SIN, YES OR NO?

Please open this session in prayer

Now that you know the Father, the Son, and the Holy Spirit lives inside you, can you continue in sin? What does scripture say about this?

_____

_____

_____

_____

_____

Did Jesus say anything about this?

_____

_____

_____

_____

_____

Can we really continue in known and persistent sin and be (submitted) believers in Christ? But we remain sinners, and we make mistakes; what are we to do?

—From Milk to Meat

_____

_____

_____

_____

_____

How about we see what the word of God from Jesus says directly.

Jesus answered them, Verily, verily, I say unto you, *Whosoever committeth sin is the servant of sin.*

John 8:34

Do you have any other verses that might shed some light on this?

_____

_____

_____

_____

So what does sin do in our lives?

_____

_____

_____

_____

_____

What was God's plan so we can be forgiven of our sins when we do commit them?

_____

_____

_____

_____

_____

_____

Please have a discussion, if you haven't already, of the need for repentance. How often should you repent? How about forgiveness of self and others? Do you have some scriptures that confirm this need?

_____

_____

_____

_____

_____

And how or by what means is the only way God can hear us?

_____

_____

_____

_____

Some people may say that the "grace of God" covers us so all our sins are forgiven; hallelujah, I can just go off and do anything I want now as long I eventually get around to asking Him to forgive me. Oops. It really doesn't work that way. Don't try and pull out the "grace card" to continue in known sin.

—From Milk to Meat

Have you ever heard or felt you can just do what you want, and then once you ask God to forgive you, it is all okay? Really? Is that how it works? Where in scripture is that?

_____

_____

_____

_____

_____

Afterward Jesus findeth him in the temple, and said unto him, Behold, thou art made whole: *sin no more*, lest a *worse thing come unto thee.*

John 5:14

What do you think "the worse thing" may be?

_____

_____

_____

_____

For the *wages of sin is death*; but the *gift of God* is eternal life through Jesus Christ our Lord.

Romans 6:23

Death, is that the worse thing? What kind of death?

_____

_____

_____

_____

But I know Jesus and He knows me! And it is a given that we all still sin, so now what? This verse has some pretty bad consequences and seems impossible to live up to, doesn't it? Can we do this all on our own?

_____

_____

_____

_____

Here are some scriptures quoted in *From Milk to Meat*.

What shall we say then? Shall *we continue in sin, that grace may abound? God forbid. How shall we, that are dead to sin, live any longer therein?*....Knowing this, that our *old man* [*unsaved self*] is crucified with him, that the body of sin might be destroyed, that henceforth *we should not serve sin*. For he that is dead is freed from sin. Now if we be dead with Christ, we believe that we shall also live with him....*Let not sin therefore reign* [*rule*] in your mortal body, that ye should obey it in the lusts thereof. *Neither yield ye your members as instruments of unrighteousness unto sin: but yield yourselves unto God*, as those that are alive from the dead, and your members as instruments of righteousness unto God. For sin shall not have *dominion* over you: for ye are not under the law, but under grace....Being then made free from sin, ye became the *servants of righteousness*. I speak after the manner of men because of the infirmity (*weakness, frailness*) of your flesh: for as ye have yielded your members servants to uncleanness and to iniquity unto iniquity; *even so now yield your members servants to righteousness unto holiness.*

Romans 6:1–2, 6–8, 12–14, 18–19

O wretched man that I am! who shall deliver me from the body of this death? I thank God *through Jesus Christ* our Lord. So then with the mind [*mind of Christ in you*] I myself serve the law of God; but with the flesh (*your own mind/self will*) the law of sin.

Romans 7:24–25

This I say then, Walk *in the (Holy) Spirit, and ye shall not fulfill the lust of the flesh.*

Galatians 5:17

This would be a good time to discuss these scriptures that Paul so clearly laid out for us. Real pearls of wisdom and understanding are in these verses related to this concept.

_____

_____

_____

_____

_____

_____

_____

_____

_____

_____

_____

_____

_____

What would be your definition of a "carnal Christian? What does this mean?

_____

_____

_____

_____

_____

Where in scripture and in what context is carnal Christianity talked about?

_____

_____

_____

_____

_____

_____

_____

_____

_____

_____

It is not in the scope of this chapter to fully explore warfare, but spiritual warfare is related to the ability to resist the devil. Which scripture shows how we can make the devil flee? This relates to resisting temptation.

_____

_____

_____

_____

_____

_____

_____

_____

Discuss how if you truly have the Holy Spirit guiding you, you will be changed and transformed. How does this help you resist the devil and his temptations?

_____

_____

_____

_____

_____

After your transformation and change into a new person in Christ, you make a mistake, what do you do immediately? What did King David do, who made some *big* mistakes?

Do you have some things you would like to list to repent of right now? Don't share this with the group unless the Lord leads you. But be real, truthful, and sincere with the Lord. There is nothing you have done that can't be forgiven. Look at the apostle Paul; he took to prison and agreed to the killing of many Christian men and women before God *chose him* for the work of the Lord!

Final notes for discussion:

CHILDLIKE FAITH

Please open this session in prayer.

What exactly does the term childlike faith mean? What did Jesus mean when He was talking about children and childlike characteristics? It is clear that to be childlike is an important quality that Jesus absolutely wants us to have! The following scripture will be a great place to start.

"And Jesus called a little child unto him, and set him in the midst of them, And said, Verily I say unto you, Except ye be converted, and become as little children, ye shall not enter into the kingdom of heaven. Whosoever therefore shall humble himself as this little child, the same is greatest in the kingdom of heaven."

Matthew 18:2–4

We will take this scripture apart and explore the truth about what it means to have childlike faith.

—*From Milk to Meat*

What do you think childlike faith means? Please include as many descriptive words as you can, and be as complete as you can be.

_____

_____

_____

_____

_____

_____

_____

_____

_____

_____

What was Jesus' attitude toward children? What were the initial adult reactions to the children scampering to get to him? Was it different from Jesus' reaction? Why?

_____

_____

_____

_____

_____

_____

Do you believe Jesus really loves children? Do you think Jesus had fun playing with them during his time on earth? How do you think He responds toward children in heaven?

_____

_____

_____

_____

_____

_____

What are the characteristics of children that Jesus wants His adults to have? This is an important list.

_____

_____

_____

_____

_____

_____

_____

As we get older, we get more jaded, suffer hurts, and lose some things. What are some of the things we lose as we get more adult? Are they all good?

_____

_____

_____

_____

_____

_____

_____

_____

How does childlike faith relate to control of your mind and actions?

_____

_____

_____

_____

_____

_____

How do we as adults act *childish* (not childlike)? Do you think Jesus likes that? Does it win us any points with Him?

_____

_____

_____

_____

_____

_____

How does the Holy Spirit relate to our ability to have a powerful faith, a childlike faith?

_____

_____

_____

_____

_____

_____

Comment and consider how we listen, hear, and obey in order to operate (as closely as it is possible) in the perfect will of God. And how does this relate to operating in complete childlike faith? Specifically address how the Holy Spirit helps with this.

_____

_____

_____

_____

_____

_____

_____

_____

What do you think is the meaning of "except ye be converted"? Do you need to change? How does repentance play into this?

_____

_____

_____

_____

_____

_____

What is the power that allows or helps you to do this?

_____

My little children, these things write I unto you, that ye sin not. And if any man sin, we have an advocate with the Father, Jesus Christ the righteous: And he is the propitiation [*replacement*] for our sins: and not for ours only, but also for the sins of the whole world. And hereby we do know that we know him, *if we keep his commandments.*

1 John 2:1–3

For ye are all the children of God *by faith* in Christ Jesus.

Galatians 3:26

Be ye therefore followers of God, as dear children.

Ephesians 5:1

Discuss these scriptures above and how they are related to being childlike in faith, our salvation and sin.

_____

_____

_____

_____

_____

_____

_____

Comment on the phrase in scripture, "become as little children." What does it therefore mean? How does this relate to truly trusting Jesus for all things? Are we to figure things out or trust our Lord to lead us? How is our trying to figure things out (in general) not operating in childlike faith?

_____

_____

_____

_____

_____

_____

In *From Milk to Meat,* I give an example of how a child would operate in a loving home. Describe your thoughts on how a well-disciplined and loved child would act.

_____

_____

_____

_____

_____

_____

How would the parents react when this child throws a temper tantrum or makes a big error? Will the parents make any allowance for mistakes? Does it change the love for the child at all? How does parental disciplinary action come into this? What is the motivation of the parent to discipline and correct a child?

_____

_____

_____

_____

_____

_____

_____

_____

_____

It is now time to consider the meaning of the verse, "We shall not enter into the kingdom of heaven." Did Jesus *really* say this? What is the true *significance* of this statement? And how specifically do childlike characteristics enter into this?

_____

_____

_____

_____

_____

_____

Below is a good verse to help clarify some of the above questions.

Verily I say unto you, Whosoever shall not receive the kingdom of God as a little child, he shall not enter therein.

Mark 10:15

The next verses relate to being a carnal Christian. Is it okay for us to just do what we want?

Therefore, brethren, we are debtors, not to the flesh, to live after the flesh. *For if ye live after the flesh, ye shall die*: but if ye through the Spirit do mortify [put to death] the deeds of the body, ye shall live.

Romans 8:12–13

For they that are *after the flesh* do mind the things of the flesh; but they that are after the Spirit the things of the Spirit. For *to be carnally minded is death*; but to be spiritually minded is life and peace. Because the carnal mind is enmity against God: for it is not subject to the law of God, neither indeed can be. So then they that are in the flesh cannot please God. But *ye are not in the flesh, but in the Spirit*, if so be that the *Spirit of God dwell in you*. Now if any man have not the Spirit of Christ, he is none of his. And if Christ be in you, the body is dead because of sin; but the Spirit is life because of righteousness.

Romans 8:5–10

Notes on these scriptures:

_____
_____
_____
_____
_____
_____
_____

Below is a scripture relating to conforming to the things of this world or our "flesh." What are we to do? How should we walk in the perfect will of the Lord?

> And be not conformed to this world: but be ye *transformed* by the *renewing of your mind*, that ye may prove (*establish*) what is that good, and acceptable, and *perfect, will of God.*
>
> Romans 12: 2

_____

_____

_____

_____

_____

_____

_____

_____

What does the Lord have to say about our being holy? Include scripture not only included from the book *From Milk to Meat,* but other scripture verses as well. Then discuss personal holiness.

_____

_____

_____

_____

_____

_____

Will you have real and perceptible changes in your life as the Holy Spirit is given place in your life? Support this with scripture. What will it look like for you?

_____

_____

_____

_____

_____

_____

_____

_____

_____

_____

The last part of the opening scripture is about being humble. Why is that so important? How is this related to childlike faith?

_____

_____

_____

_____

_____

_____

_____

_____

Why does Jesus ask us to *believe and obey* in childlike faith?

_____

_____

_____

_____

_____

Is it really this simple? State what Jesus said about how to become great in the kingdom of heaven? Do we really and truly *want and desire* to be great in His kingdom? Why should we?

_____

_____

_____

_____

_____

_____

_____

_____

Do you need to ask Jesus to help you with your childlike faith? Do you understand or believe you can look at your walk with Jesus as simply as a child does? What would you like Jesus to help you with in regard to this? Then just ask him!

_____

_____

_____

_____

_____

_____

_____

My prayer is you will re-read this and the references as many times as needed and set this in your heart. As you operate in childlike faith with the power of the Holy Spirit in true humility, it will become even more fun and exciting as God opens up more and more of His goodness and joy for you.

—From Milk to Meat

Here is space for final notes on the discussion for this chapter.

_____

_____

_____

_____

_____

_____

_____

_____

_____

_____

_____

FOLLOW ME AND ARE WE LISTENING

P lease open this session in prayer.

What does Jesus mean when He says many times "Follow me" in the Word? Is this optional? What will your life look like if you truly "follow me"?

If any man serve me, let him follow me; and where I am, there shall also my servant be: if any man serve me, him will my Father honour.

John 12:26

This verse is pretty clear about what it means to serve Jesus. If we want to serve Jesus and be honored by God Himself, we need to follow Jesus.

—*From Milk to Meat*

So what do you think Jesus meant when He said so many times in scripture, "Follow me"?

_____

_____

_____

_____

_____

_____

_____

Is it optional or mandatory? What happens if you don't follow Jesus?

_____

_____

_____

_____

_____

_____

Does it mean to follow Him only when it is convenient or easy?

_____

_____

_____

_____

Why is the connector "if" used so many times in scripture? Does this mean things are not for certain unless we *do* something? Make a list of things that we must do in our walk with Jesus.

_____

_____

_____

_____

_____

_____

_____

_____

_____

_____

Do we need to be committed to following Jesus? What does that look like to you?

_____

_____

_____

_____

_____

Will it always be fun and pleasant to follow Jesus? What things can we expect to see if we truly follow Jesus? There are wonderful and painful things (persecution from many sources, including your own family for a time) that can be included in this list!

_____

_____

_____

_____

_____

_____

Does Jesus want us to be committed and to stay the course or stand for the faith? Where is this spoken of in scripture?

_____

_____

_____

_____

_____

Does giving up things mean to not care about those things or people at all? Discuss how this could be "giving them (whatever it or who it is) to God and letting him deal with them?" Discuss and relate how this is a spiritual commitment, which has some real physical aspects as well.

_____

_____

_____

_____

_____

_____

_____

Discuss how we need to hear and obey His will for us. How do we hear His will for us?

_____

_____

_____

_____

_____

Will Jesus provide for our needs? Will He provide for all of our wants or desires while on this earth? What scriptures support this?

_____

_____

_____

_____

_____

Then said Jesus unto his disciples, If any man will come after me, let him deny himself, and *take up his cross, and follow me.* For whosoever will save his life shall lose it: and whosoever will *lose his life for my sake* shall find it.

Matthew 16:24–25

What does it mean to you to "deny yourself," "take up the cross," and "follow me"?

_____

_____

_____

_____

_____

What will change in you as you give up your personal desires and seek His desires completely? How does this look to you?

_____

_____

_____

_____

_____

Are we perfect? Does God allow for this, that we will make mistakes along the way? What are we to do when we realized we made a mistake or sinned?

_____

_____

_____

_____

Is our Lord concerned with only the "big things," or does He care about the smallest detail of our life? Support this with scripture.

_____

_____

_____

_____

Can we look back and re-engage in old patterns and lifestyles? What is the risk if we do? What scriptures give warning about this?

_____

_____

_____

_____

_____

What tool did the Father and Jesus give us to help us with following Him?

_____

_____

_____

_____

This would be a good time to list characteristics of those who are following Jesus. Make a list of them; this is well stated in scripture.

_____

_____

_____

_____

_____

_____

_____

Do you truly want to follow Jesus now? Ask Him to help you, teach you, and send more of His Holy Spirit to help and guide you. Then repent when you "oops" immediately, and get back on the horse! The Father and Son love us more than we can imagine, and we get to love Him back! Praise the Lord.

Discussion notes.

_____

_____

_____

_____

_____

Are we listening to God all the time? Are we sensitive to His speaking to us in everything we do, every breath we take, every action we do? Do we need to listen to Him, and if so, why? What are the consequences to our walk in faith if we don't? This lesson can't fully answer these questions but will get a start on them at least.

—From Milk to Meat

Read the above paragraph; what does it say to you?

_____

_____

_____

_____

_____

_____

_____

What scriptures can you find to support this discussion?

_____

_____

_____

Do you truly believe this is very important for our walk with the Lord? What happens if we aren't listening to the Lord?

_____

_____

_____

_____

_____

Do we all at times hear the Lord, then "I think about it," and "do what I want," and it is not in the perfect will of God? How do you know when it happens?

_____

_____

_____

_____

_____

Do these lessons or tests the Lord gives us, and we may fail at, always have eternal significance? Could they possibly be the Lord's "teaching tool" for us as we learn to listen, hear, and obey? How did we learn things as children, or how do our children learn? Are mistakes that we learn from a major part of learning?

_____

_____

_____

_____

_____

_____

_____

What should we do as soon as we *know* we made an "oops"?

_____

_____

_____

_____

_____

This may, in many cases, be called a feeling, impression, or just intuition. It may be angels guarding us. But I will present this is God speaking to us directly through the Holy Spirit living in us for those who belong to Him.

—From Milk to Meat

Now, what are the ways the Lord will let you know things?

_____

_____

_____

_____

_____

God will use this method of speaking to us to expose things He wants us to know. Only if we remain childlike in belief and trust with immediate obedience when we hear are we operating in His will and then get the full message and result He wants us to have. And it may be in regard to things that are very important and serious. Do you want to ask Jesus to help you to improve your listening abilities? Then simply ask Him for more. Ask for more of whatever from His heavenly resources you desire and require to operate fully in His will for your life. He wants to give us gifts and blessings; simply ask for them framed in His righteousness for His glory. And repent and ask for forgiveness as soon as you realize you have failed again! Then our Lord will be able to help us in our walk of faith with Him.

—From Milk to Meat

Final notes:

_____

_____

_____

_____

_____

_____

_____

_____

THE RICH MAN AND LOWEST
INCOME MONTH EVER

Please open this time in prayer.

Did Jesus talk about money in scripture? Why do you think that is?

_____

_____

_____

_____

_____

> And these are they which are *sown among thorns*; such as hear the word, And the cares of this world, and the deceitfulness of riches, and the lusts of other things entering in, choke the word, and it becometh unfruitful.
>
> Mark 4:18–19

This is a powerful verse. It is very pertinent to many people at this time, especially in the rich nations of the world. It is ultimately a prime cause of carnal Christianity. Discuss this verse and what you think it means. Why does a persecuted church body grow and thrive? Is it the same in a rich church body?

_____

_____

_____

_____

_____

I know thy works, that thou art neither cold nor hot: I would thou wert cold or hot. So then because *thou art lukewarm*, and neither cold nor hot, I will spue (*vigorously or forcefully vomit or eject*) thee out of my mouth. *Because thou sayest, I am rich*, and increased with goods, and *have need of nothing*; and knowest not that thou art *wretched*, and *miserable*, and poor, and *blind, and naked*:

Revelation 3:15–17

The above verse was *for me personally* the verse preached by my pastor in April 2011, that got me to say, "Yes, Lord, I will go with you now. Forgive me!" I made a choice, and then the process started that led to what is now evident with how He is using me for His glory at this time. What does this verse say to you?

_____

_____

_____

_____

_____

List some positive things that money can do.

_____

_____

_____

_____

_____

_____

List some things that an excess of money can cause.

_____

_____

_____

_____

_____

_____

But they that will be *rich fall into temptation and a snare*, and into *many foolish and hurtful lusts, which drown men in destruction and perdition*. For the love of money is the root of all evil: which while some coveted after, they have *erred from the faith*, and pierced themselves through with *many sorrows*. But thou, O man of God, *flee these things*; and follow after righteousness, godliness, faith, love, patience, meekness....

Charge them that are rich in this world, that they be not highminded [*prideful*], nor trust in uncertain riches, but in the living God, who giveth us richly all things to enjoy; That they do good, that they be rich in good works, ready to distribute, willing to communicate; Laying up in store for themselves a good foundation against the time to come, that they may lay hold on eternal life.

1 Timothy 6:9–11, 17–19

How can money be a snare and a temptation?

_____

_____

_____

_____

_____

What are the hurtful things money can cause people to do?

_____

_____

_____

_____

_____

How can money or striving for it cause you to reject your faith?

_____

_____

_____

_____

_____

Why do you see media reports of very rich people committing suicide? Shouldn't they be happy since they have every luxury of life and have all their wants met? What do you think is missing? Have you heard the stories of a "Mexico youth mission trip" and how amazed the youth are when they come back about how loving, generous, and happy these *very* poor people are!

_____

_____

_____

_____

_____

_____

Do you trust God to provide *completely* for your daily needs? How about for your retirement?

_____

_____

_____

_____

What kinds of things could be the "many sorrows" the scripture is referring to?

_____

_____

_____

Jesus said unto him, If thou wilt be perfect, *go and sell* that thou hast, and give to the poor, and thou shalt have treasure in heaven: and come and follow me. But when the young man heard that saying, he *went away sorrowful*: for he had great possessions.

Matthew 19:21–23

Discuss what this parable from Jesus means. Is it pertinent to us today?

_____

_____

_____

_____

_____

Why did Jesus ask the rich man to sell all? Did Jesus need the money? What did Jesus see that was the blockage or stumbling block of this young man to entering into the kingdom of God? What was Jesus *really* asking the young rich man to do?

_____

_____

_____

_____

_____

Having therefore these promises, dearly beloved, let us *cleanse ourselves* from all filthiness of the flesh and spirit, *perfecting holiness* in the *fear of God*.

2 Corinthians 7:1

Read up and down a bit from this verse in 2 Corinthians 7. In what way does this speak to you about how God views our use of money and wealth? Proverbs speaks much about money matters, look up verses there. There are many pearls in this verse!

_____

_____

_____

_____

_____

_____

_____

_____

What is more important for you? Jesus or anything else? *Anything* at all? Where in scripture does it say that Jesus wants all of our heart and soul and mind? Can we give Him only the parts we want to give Him?

_____

_____

_____

_____

_____

What is our reward if we will follow and serve Jesus at this scripturally true commitment level?

_____

_____

_____

_____

_____

What is the penalty if we don't?

_____

_____

_____

_____

Comment on the phrase from scripture, "The Lord searches your heart." What do you think this really means?

_____

_____

_____

_____

_____

_____

Do we have to take a vow of poverty to serve Jesus? Or is he searching our hearts as to what our true and deep motivation to really serve Him is?

_____

_____

_____

_____

_____

_____

Enter ye in at the strait gate: for *wide* is the gate, and *broad* is the way, that *leadeth to destruction*, and many there be which go in thereat: *Because strait is the gate, and narrow is the way, which leadeth unto life*, and few there be that find it.

Matthew 7:13–14

We've discussed this before in prior chapters, but what is the wide gate, and what is the narrow gate? And how is this related to striving for wealth or things of the world? What is the penalty for taking the common, easy, wide gate?

_____

_____

_____

_____

_____

_____

And how does this relate to "flesh desires"? Does it have a correlation with carnal Christianity?

_____

_____

_____

_____

_____

_____

And again I say unto you, it is easier for a *camel* to go through the *eye of a needle*, than for a rich man to enter into the kingdom of God. When his disciples heard it, they were exceedingly amazed, saying, Who then can be saved? But Jesus beheld them, and said unto them, With men this is impossible; but *with God all things are possible.*

Matthew 19:24–26

But every *man is tempted, when he is drawn away of his own lust*, and enticed [*trapped*]. Then when lust hath conceived (*thought about*), it bringeth forth sin: and sin, when it is finished, bringeth forth (*eternal*) death. Do not err [*make mistakes*], my beloved brethren.

James 1:14–16

Comment on how these scriptures relate to lust for wealth or fleshly desires. And if we fail outside the love of Jesus (salvation and our true repentance and transformation), what happens?

_____

_____

_____

_____

_____

_____

_____

_____

_____

How is it possible to fully put your trust in the Lord and have money as well? What must your attitude be? What must your life look like?

_____

_____

_____

_____

_____

_____

_____

_____

Does it say anywhere in scripture we are to be poor only? Does it say anywhere, "If you have money, you are bad in my eyes"? Doesn't Jesus want us to be filled abundantly? So how do we do this? How can we have money and not sin? What does that look like? Is it easy? What are the traps as you look at it from your life?

_____

_____

_____

_____

_____

_____

_____

_____

_____

I beseech you therefore, brethren, by the mercies of God, that ye present your bodies a living sacrifice, holy, acceptable unto God, which is your reasonable service. And be not conformed to this world: but *be ye transformed by the renewing of your mind*, that ye may prove what is that good, and acceptable, and perfect, will of God.

Romans 12:1–2

We've seen this verse already in these studies, but it is pertinent to this lesson as well. Discuss how this verse relates to giving to God control of all our resources. How does the Holy Spirit enter into this?

_____

_____

_____

_____

_____

_____

_____

_____

Did Jesus state He knows our needs and will provide everything? Do you have faith and believe that completely, even in hard circumstances? Find and write the scriptures, then discuss it.

_____

_____

_____

_____

_____

_____

_____

_____

_____

Can you do this journey? Thread the eye of the needle all on your own? Who is available to help and guide you along this path and walk?

_____

_____

_____

_____

_____

Do you see how you can have more fun, real joy, and fulfillment chasing after what God wants you to do rather than chasing after your own personal wants, dreams, and plans?

_____

_____

_____

_____

_____

Is it really this simple? That you simply listen, hear, and obey what God wants you to do; do that in *childlike faith* and you will have joy and contentment. This is living the transformed life for Jesus. How would that look for you? How would you use the money the Lord has given you?

_____

_____

_____

_____

_____

_____

_____

August 2012 was a record month for income in my medical practice, praise the Lord. It was the one-year anniversary of my transformation by Jesus and of giving my house, my medical practice, and my finances to God. And it was the lowest net income I have ever made, absolutely nothing for the month! The total receipts from my medical practice were not enough to even cover office expenses for the month, much less any left over for personal salary.

—*From Milk to Meat*

This is a quote from the book, and this reality was a bit of a shock to me. The timing was about a year into my walking closely in the Holy Spirit with Jesus. Interesting, huh?

_____

_____

_____

_____

How is it possible to rejoice when circumstances just keep on getting hard and harder?

_____

_____

_____

_____

_____

Why does our Lord allow this?

_____

_____

_____

_____

_____

Does a loving father discipline (or prune) His children to help them (or to make better fruit)? How might this look spiritually?

_____

_____

_____

_____

_____

_____

_____

_____

_____

Will the Lord allow testing to see how you will do? Is this fun? What do you think is God's purpose in allowing this?

_____

_____

_____

_____

Discuss in detail the real life faith story of Abraham and Isaac as a sacrifice. Was this a test from the Lord? Why did God do this, and what was the result?

_____

_____

_____

_____

_____

Did Abraham believe and have faith in what God asked him to do? Did he have doubts that this was the perfect will of God for him? He obeyed, and God honored him. What does this say to us about obeying what the Lord asks us to do once we are sure it is His perfect will?

_____

_____

_____

_____

_____

Are we allowed to doubt? Are we allowed to bicker? Are we allowed to figure it all out? Are we allowed to make contingency plans for God's plan? How would a loved child respond?

_____

_____

_____

_____

_____

How does this relate to childlike faith and trust as we do the will of the Lord?

_____

_____

_____

_____

_____

We are also to test in the Spirit. What does this mean? Are there false prophets or false messages? How do we tell the difference?

_____

_____

_____

_____

_____

_____

_____

Did Job ever curse God even when all was taken from him? What does that show us?

_____

_____

_____

_____

_____

So if you are undergoing some testing, rejoice in it and accept it for exactly what it is: God's best for you. Now that does not mean we are to just accept things that are unacceptable in all respects (like physical abuse). We may need to take action to change some things.

Seek the Lord, ask Him what He wants you to do: confirm it with 1–2 others that hear from the Lord then move and act on that information as He gives it to you. This is how we can operate in a mature fashion in the body of Christ and in childlike faith with the joy of the Lord in difficult circumstances.

—From Milk to Meat

Notes for final discussion:

_____

_____

_____

_____

_____

_____

_____

_____

_____

_____

_____

_____

_____

_____

_____

WHAT ARE TONGUES ABOUT?

Please open this session in prayer.

What has been your personal observation or direct encounter with tongues?

_____

_____

_____

_____

_____

_____

Do you have any firm thoughts or concepts at this time about tongues?

_____

_____

_____

_____

This teaching may be controversial and subject to differences of opinion. It has been a real plan of Satan to cause confusion about this gift of the Holy Spirit. But this gift of the Holy Spirit is real and in operation in the body of Christ at this time. What does scripture say about restricting tongues in the church? Where is the scripture?

_____

_____

_____

So if tongues are not to be restricted, we need to learn from the word and the Holy Spirit what tongues are all about and what this gift isn't.

If you are having a hard time with the topic of tongues from past experience and teachings, please stop and pray now. Ask the Lord Jesus and the Spirit of God to help you to understand what He wants you to know, and open your heart and mind to receive what He wants you to see and hear.

Test what you hear and learn in the Holy Spirit for truth. Don't take a person's word as a final authority, but be assured of truth when it is spoken or written as a teaching. Do not take what is my opinion from this book and take it as the truth without testing and confirming it through the power of the Holy Spirit and what the Word says. This teaching may seem to be controversial, but this information needs to be taught.

_____

_____

_____

_____

_____

Isn't this fun? As you are working through these chapters, it is my prayer that the Lord is revealing truth after truth to you through the power of the Holy Spirit. Another of those truths to now explore further is a manifestation of the Holy Spirit commonly called tongues. It is speaking in a real language directly to God that you have no prior knowledge or learning of from prior experience. It is a real language that you don't know (unless interpreted) what is being said. It is direct communication, or communion, between God residing in you through the Holy Spirit and the Father in heaven. This is simply one of the manifestations of the Holy Spirit and is expressed when the person involved is giving free release of their body for the Holy Spirit to speak through. It is not about us; it is about the release and effect of the Holy Spirit in His Body of Christ (and us individually) for His glory. It is not about tongues as such; it is about Jesus and the free release of the Holy Spirit! There is much confusion about tongues. It is my prayer that this teaching chapter will help reduce confusion over what tongues really are.

—From Milk to Meat

What does the author list as the two types of tongues?

1. _____

2. _____

Do you agree? Discuss and takes notes below as to your reasoning.

_____

_____

_____

_____

_____

If you don't think there are two types of tongues, support it with scripture here, and discuss it. Ask our Lord to reveal to you what He wants you to know.

_____

_____

_____

_____

_____

The first type of tongues, your personal prayer language, is meant for conversation between you and God directly. Discuss scriptures and statements related to this in *From Milk to Meat*.

_____

_____

_____

_____

_____

_____

And He said unto them, Go ye into all the world, and preach the gospel to every creature. *He that believeth and is baptized shall be saved*; but he that believeth not shall be damned. And *these signs shall follow* them that believe; In my name shall they cast out devils [*do deliverance, a very big topic*]; *they shall speak with new tongues.*

Mark 16:15–17

What does this verse say to you? This is from Jesus directly!

_____

_____

_____

_____

_____

_____

Is there a connection between being a believer and the things that a believer will now do as a result?

_____

_____

_____

_____

_____

Tongues are between you and God, and it is meant for conversation (or direct communion) between you and God…. This is the proof that the Holy Spirit resides in you …. From the reference above, it is clear if you believe, you shall speak with new tongues…. Your personal prayer directly with God through tongues is important for all of us as followers of Jesus. It is again direct and perfect prayer between God in us and God in heaven. God gave to each person their own prayer language for our own edification. This will express as tongues, or speech, to those that have an overflowing of the Spirit residing in them and have released Him to speak. Reread this last sentence, please; it is the key to this whole teaching.

—*From Milk to Meat*

There is much information in the above reference. Please discuss it piece by piece and write your notes below. Please support your discussion answers with scripture as needed.

_____

_____

_____

_____

_____

_____

_____

_____

_____

_____

_____

_____

_____

_____

_____

_____

Read in Acts and discuss how the *only proof* the "church of Jerusalem" required to accept the gentiles as fellow believers in Christ was they "received the Holy Spirit like we had." And that was they spoke in tongues. It was not proof of lasting fruit, righteous living, or anything else, simply this gift from God. Look up these verses and discuss it.

_____

_____

_____

_____

_____

_____

The Lord talks about rivers, overflowing, and streams in relation to the word and the Holy Spirit. Why do you think this is?

_____

_____

_____

_____

_____

_____

Is this excess or overflowing of the Holy Spirit from us the *light and fire* of the Holy Spirit from our *relationship* with Jesus? Discuss this concept. Do we need to be refilled constantly so the Spirit of God in us can flow out, share, impact, and impart blessings to others?

_____

_____

_____

_____

_____

_____

_____

_____

Are we to pray in the language God gave to us? How frequently? What scripture supports this? (Look at the scriptures in *From Milk to Meat*.) Can you find others?

_____

_____

_____

_____

_____

_____

_____

What other spiritual benefits come to us when we pray in the Spirit to God?

_____

_____

_____

_____

_____

_____

And *these signs shall follow* them that believe; In my name shall they cast out devils [*do deliverance, a very big topic*]; *they shall speak with new tongues.*

Mark 16:17

Yes, this was quoted earlier in this session, but let us look at from another angle. What does this scripture say to you now?

_____

_____

_____

_____

_____

_____

Is this verse as relevant now as it was when Jesus spoke it? Why?

_____

_____

_____

_____

_____

_____

Do you think Satan wants to confuse people about this truth? Why do you think that might be true? Comment on that.

_____

_____

_____

_____

_____

_____

The next two verses are the commands that we are to pray in our prayer language and some clarification about what it actually is and why we need to do this. When we pray in the Spirit, we talk directly to God, and this "builds us up." Who wouldn't want to do this? I can't see any negative or downside to this, do you?

—*From Milk to Meat*

He that speaketh in an unknown tongue edifieth himself; and let him *speak to himself, and to God.*

1 Corinthians 14:4

But ye, beloved, building up yourselves on your most holy faith, *praying in the Holy Ghost.*

Jude 20

Comment on what these two verses say to you?

_____

_____

_____

_____

_____

_____

Discuss the fact that the Holy Spirit is part of the trinity (Godhead) of God and *is* God. That God gave the Holy Spirit to reside in us, making us a temple of God. The Holy Spirit is a real personality and can communicate with us by and through the use of our tongue. Discuss this and about the related teachings in *From Milk to Meat*.

_____

_____

_____

_____

_____

_____

_____

_____

What? know ye not that *your body is the temple* of the *Holy Ghost* which is in you, which ye have *of God*, and ye are not your own? For ye are bought with a price: therefore *glorify God in your body, and in your spirit, which are God's*.

1 Corinthians 6:19–20

Discuss this verse above.

_____

_____

_____

_____

_____

The second type of tongues is the one spoken in group settings that require interpretation. This is a prophetically based gift of the Spirit. This use of tongues is a gifting that not everybody has, unlike your personal prayer language that every Spirit-overfilled believer has. The language itself may or may not be the same as your prayer language.

—*From Milk to Meat*

Please discuss the above statement from the book. Read around it in the book to get more clarity for the discussion. Please read the related scriptures and find more as you desire. What is God talking to you about this truth?

_____

_____

_____

_____

_____

_____

Is this use of tongues orderly? Why?

_____

_____

_____

_____

Sometimes, the Spirit of God will manifest in *odd* ways to our way of thinking. But whatever is seen (shaking, "collapse in the Spirit," etc.) will be able to be *discerned* as real and from God. Comment on your thoughts on this. Have you seen these manifestations personally? How did they affect you, or what did you think about it?

_____

_____

_____

_____

_____

_____

_____

_____

_____

What does Paul say in 1 Corinthians 14 about the use of tongues (or the gifts in general) in corporate settings (church)? And why was this explained so clearly? God is orderly, and so is to be the use of the gifts He gave to us! The Holy Spirit cannot be restricted in His free operation either. And this is the balancing act so many people find themselves in. It is so very important to not grieve and quench the Holy Spirit by trying to "control" His movements in believers.

Again, this movement of the Holy Spirit is to be orderly, which is different from "controlled." And leaders need to be discerning to be sure it is the Holy Spirit moving, and not just "flesh" that sort of "looks" like a "Spirit (of what and who?)" moving. There is way too much to discuss at this time from these last couple paragraphs, with all its meanings. Maybe this could be the topic for another book or teaching later?

This may be an "interesting" discussion in the group now! See what the Lord shows you about what has just been elaborated on.

_____

_____

_____

_____

_____

_____

_____

_____

_____

What are some of the ways the Lord may use the gift of tongues in worship? Will you object to the Lord having you speak this way? Will it embarrass you? Is it fun to worship like this?

_____

_____

_____

_____

_____

_____

_____

_____

How does discernment of what is happening play into this in a corporate setting? Is everything always from God, or can Satan insert his stuff at times and make it look like the Holy Spirit? Really? Most definitely, "yes." Discuss these thoughts now.

_____

_____

_____

_____

_____

_____

_____

Praying in the Holy Spirit (tongues) are used in healing, warfare, and deliverance. Let us leave that topic for another day, unless brought up by the group for discussion.

_____

_____

_____

_____

_____

_____

_____

There are many people clearly filled with the Holy Spirit and walking with Jesus who haven't been able to release their personal audible prayer language yet. It is being blocked by personal choices or lack of understanding of what tongues really is by the person.

—From Milk to Meat

What is this about? Having the gift of the Holy Spirit and not using it? Releasing your personal prayer language? How does this occur?

_____

_____

_____

_____

_____

_____

_____

_____

The following scripture is the key to releasing your prayer language I believe. Why? Because it revolves around the *key* of childlike faith and humility.

> And Jesus called a little child unto him, and set him in the midst of them, And said, Verily I say unto you, *Except ye be converted, and become as little children, ye shall not enter into the kingdom of heaven.* Whosoever therefore shall *humble* himself as this little child, the same is greatest in the kingdom of heaven.
>
> Matthew 18:2–4

In *From Milk to Meat*, how does the author state that your prayer language can be released? Can the release occur at the time of your salvation? Does it usually?

_____

_____

_____

_____

_____

_____

_____

_____

How does childlike faith come into release of your prayer language?

_____

_____

_____

_____

_____

_____

What does the Lord speak to you about the number of times "childlike faith" is needed for something to fully implement in our walk in the kingdom of God?

_____

_____

_____

_____

_____

Why do you need to be humble as well?

_____

_____

_____

_____

_____

Does this sound complex or impossible to do? It does seem rather simple, but is it easy? Ask the Lord to help you with your *faith* to believe in the things you can't see.

_____

_____

_____

_____

_____

Wow, that was a long and "interesting" teaching! Pray now for the Holy Spirit to teach and instruct you in what He wants you to receive.

Are you ready now to release your prayer language?

Then ask Jesus to overfill you with the Holy Spirit and to release to Him the control of your tongue so He can speak through you. It really is that simple. But you must have belief, faith, and trust like a child. *Don't let the adult in you block this release.* You can pray this as a group, with laying on of hands, or just between you and the Lord in complete privacy. Any method works. The Lord is waiting for you to do this so He can talk back and forth (or commune) intimately with you!

Blessings!

Final notes for discussion:

_____

_____

_____

_____

_____

_____

_____

_____

_____

_____

_____

_____

_____

_____

_____

_____

HOW SHOULD I PRAY FOR
EFFECTIVE PRAYER?

Please open this session in prayer.

What would be your definition of an effective prayer?

_____

_____

_____

_____

_____

_____

What specific characteristics do think a truly effective prayer would have?

_____

_____

_____

_____

_____

_____

The verse below, the Lord's Prayer, is what the disciples of Jesus asked Him to show them what a proper prayer would look like.

Our Father which art in heaven,
Hallowed be thy name.
Thy kingdom come.

Thy will be done in earth, as it is in heaven.
Give us this day our daily bread.
And forgive us our debts, as we forgive our debtors.
And lead us not into temptation, But deliver us from evil:
For thine is the kingdom, And the power,
And the glory, for ever.
Amen.

Matthew 6:7–13

Why is this prayer a good model for us when we pray?

_____
_____
_____
_____
_____

How do we pray so that our prayers are a direct hit and are effective? How do we not miss in our prayer? What factors can block or impair our prayer?

How do we not have a feel-good prayer, but an effective and holy prayer that God is pleased with and will answer right now?

—From Milk to Meat

Discuss the importance of worship in our prayers. Why is this central to our prayer?

_____
_____
_____
_____
_____
_____

Did God send us ministering angels? What do they do?

_____
_____
_____
_____
_____

Do we need to pray to accomplish what God wants or what *we* want for our personal benefit? At times, can they be different or the same? How so?

_____

_____

_____

_____

_____

_____

It is right that we pray what we want, but what is the *motivation* behind what we are asking for? Is it in God's perfect will for what He wants us to be doing? What if what we are praying for isn't in His perfect will?

_____

_____

_____

_____

_____

_____

All the ways of a man are clean in his own eyes; but the Lord weigheth the spirits (*sees the 'real' motivation*). Commit thy works unto the Lord, and thy thoughts shall be established....Every one that is proud in heart is an abomination to the Lord: though hand join in hand, he shall not be unpunished....A man's heart deviseth his way: but the Lord directeth his steps....There is a way that seemeth right unto a man, but the *end* thereof are the *ways of death*

Proverbs 16:2–3, 5, 9, 25

Discuss the above verse. There are many parts to it that relate to a correct attitude for prayer requests. The motivation for the prayer is what God weighs or evaluates.

_____

_____

_____

_____

_____

Do you have an area that is "my stuff" that you are trying to keep control of? What does God think of that? Do you trust God for all your "daily bread"?

_____

_____

_____

_____

_____

_____

In the Lord's Prayer, what does it say about the need to forgive and be forgiven? How important is forgiveness for effective prayer?

_____

_____

_____

_____

_____

_____

Jesus knows all about Satan and temptation and has given us a way to resist the devil and his ways. Is this important in prayer? Why?

_____

_____

_____

_____

_____

Is our prayer framed to absolutely and completely bring glory to God? Why? What did Jesus do for us that He gets all the credit for the work that we do in love for Him? What does God say if we try to take His glory?

_____

_____

_____

_____

_____

If we give Glory to the Son, does that bring Glory to the Father? Where is this discussed in the scriptures? Please look them up and discuss this. Why is this so important for us to understand?

_____

_____

_____

_____

_____

Read James 4:2–4. Do you think some of the things listed there will block effective prayer? Are the things talked about holy and righteous? James is talking about believers (not walking in the will of the Lord or carnal), not the unsaved!

> Ye lust, and have not: ye kill, and desire to have, and cannot obtain: ye fight and war, yet ye have not, because ye ask not. Ye ask, and receive not, *because ye ask amiss,* that ye *may consume it upon your lusts.* Ye adulterers and adulteresses, know ye not that the friendship of the world is *enmity* with God? whosoever therefore will be a *friend of the world is the enemy of God.*
>
> James 4:2–4

This is a pretty harsh scripture, isn't it? Did James really say "enemy of God"? But this scripture is here for teaching and to help us become better. So what do these verses really say to you?

_____

_____

_____

_____

_____

_____

What things have you discovered that can block or impede prayer?

_____

_____

_____

_____

_____

Would God answer anything asked of Him that was unholy, unrighteous, or not pure? Discuss this.

_____

_____

_____

_____

_____

_____

_____

_____

_____

_____

_____

Confess your faults one to another, and *pray* one for another, that ye may *be healed.* The *effectual fervent prayer of a righteous man availeth much.*

James 5:16

Take heed, brethren, lest there be in any of you an evil heart of unbelief, in departing from the living God. But *exhort one another daily*, while it is called To-day; *lest any of you be hardened through the deceitfulness of sin*

Hebrews 3:12–13

Why would it be important that we be a part of a body of Christ? Scripture tells us to come together for prayer, to praise Him, for our support and accountability to each other. Why would this be essential to a healthy spiritual life?

_____

_____

_____

_____

_____

_____

_____

And all things, whatsoever ye shall ask in prayer, believing, ye shall receive.

Matthew 21:22

Why do we need to *believe* when we ask for anything in prayer? Are we allowed to be afraid? If we are afraid, what does that say about trust in the Lord? Do you have any idea how many times in scripture "Do not fear" or an equivalent is written? Why would it be in scripture so often? What is God telling us about fearing or to be afraid?

_____

_____

_____

_____

_____

_____

_____

_____

_____

_____

And whatsoever ye shall ask in my name, that will I do, that the *Father may be glorified in the Son. If* ye shall ask any thing in my name, I will do it. *If* ye love me, *keep* my commandments. *And* I will pray the Father, and he shall give you another Comforter, that he may abide with you forever.

John 14:13–16

Why do we need to ask in Jesus' name? Why does it have to do with His death, His blood, and then His glory?

_____

_____

_____

_____

_____

_____

_____

_____

Discuss how those very important connector words *if* and *and* are used in this verse above? Why is it so important? Does this mean some things in the kingdom of God are contingent on what *we do?* And what does *that* mean to me personally?

_____

_____

_____

_____

_____

_____

Discuss how when we pray, it all comes together: listen, hear, obey, follow me, die to self, and use the gifts of the Holy Spirit you have received. And discuss how if we do this, it leads to real peace and joy.

_____

_____

_____

_____

_____

_____

_____

_____

If ye abide in me, *and* my words abide in you, *ye shall ask what ye will, and it shall be done unto you.* Herein is my Father glorified, that *ye bear much fruit;* so shall ye be my disciples.

John 15:7–8

And I say unto you, Ask, and it shall be given you; seek, and ye shall find; knock, and it shall be opened unto you. For every one that asketh receiveth; and he that seeketh findeth; and to him that knocketh it shall be opened.

Luke 11:9

You must diligently search, seek, and knock. You must be in the Word and put that wisdom into your heart so it can affect your actions. You must seek to understand God and worship Him fully. For those who do this, you will know by the Holy Spirit what to ask in God's will, and He will grant it.

—From Milk to Meat

In what way does this speak to you?

_____

_____

_____

_____

_____

_____

_____

Now to complete the topic of effective prayer, let's go back to the Old Testament and read a psalm of David. David knew how to pray! Read this with a worshipful heart, and ask the Lord for full understanding of the truth and mysteries locked up in this psalm. It is an amazing prayer. Try to memorize it; it is like the Lord's Prayer in importance as a model for effective prayer. We should have it in our mind at any time ready to pray in a still moment with the Lord, or in a stressful moment of need. It just happens to be twelve lines in total, God's perfect number!

The Lord is my shepherd; I shall not want.
He maketh me to lie down in green pastures:
he leadeth me beside the still waters.
He restoreth my soul:
he leadeth me in the paths of righteousness for his name's sake.
Yea, though I walk through the valley of the shadow of death,
I will fear no evil: for thou art with me;
thy rod and thy staff they comfort me.
Thou preparest a table before me in the presence of mine enemies:
thou anointest my head with oil; my cup runneth over.
Surely goodness and mercy shall follow me all the days of my life:
and I will dwell in the house of the Lord forever.

Psalm 23

If there is time in the session, read each line separately and discuss them line by line.

1. _____

_____

2. _____

_____

3. _____
   _____

4. _____
   _____

5. _____
   _____

6. _____
   _____

7. _____
   _____

8. _____
   _____

9. _____
   _____

10. _____
    _____

11. _____
    _____

12. _____
    _____

As you apply this to your prayer life, you will see results to your prayers that will astound you! Blessings.

Final Notes:

_____
_____
_____
_____
_____
_____
_____
_____
_____
_____

CONCLUSION

I hope and pray you have benefited greatly from this workbook companion to *From Milk to Meat*. As you have progressed and now completed this workbook, I pray you have had a transformation of your mind and heart and are now getting a "supercharge" for Jesus. Now this is just a start on your path of discovery for your walk with Jesus.

I pray this study and decisions made from it will be just one of God's tools to help His body of Christ to gain the knowledge and wisdom needed for the walk with the Lord in the kingdom of God in His full power and authority to then accomplish the task the Lord has given to each of us fully in the joy of the Lord.

As you have progressed in the workbook from the basic salvation question to how to have a truly effective prayer life, you will see how simple this truly is. Pray that you will have the faith and belief to move into the next stage of your walk with Jesus.

I pray you will be a powerful light and testimony of Jesus as you walk your life from this point forward, side by side, arm in arm with Jesus.

Amen.

Included below is simply the conclusion from the original book. Blessings to you and yours!

In this book, we have certainly opened up a large number of topics, and some could have controversial aspects as they may not be widely understood and taught. I don't profess to be an all-knowledgeable Christian or to have all the answers. It is likely that as my growth in the Lord progresses, I may write and teach these lessons with a somewhat different emphasis, use additional or different scriptures, or have slightly different key points. There will likely be several books following this one to expand into more depth on the truths and topics opened in this book. But the ultimate purpose of this book is to cause people to grow in the Lord so they will be able to be the workers to help bring in the harvest of souls waiting for Jesus and the Father.

My attempt in this collection of stories and meat chapters was to provide you with a single source of information that will help you as a guidebook for your real discovery of the Holy Spirit, how to become empowered by the Holy Spirit, and the initial stages of what that means for your walk with Jesus. It worked for me as laid out, so the Lord had me share it with you. It is written from the viewpoint of a new convert who has recently been through it and has the scars to show for it! The Lord has made it clear to me there are many people like I was. With this book and scripture, the Holy Spirit can help all of us to understand what is needed to form that tight relationship with Jesus and the Father in heaven. Love!

And the teachings in this book will also have shown you how you don't need to fear the devil or any of his minions, devils, or obstructing actions or effects. When you are in a correct relationship with Jesus through the power of the Holy Spirit, Satan can't touch you!

This book will help get you started on the adventure with Jesus! You can then continue even further in your successful walk with Jesus.

So what are some key questions that would be pertinent to make sure were discussed and answered from this book?

- *Do you know Jesus at this time? Do you want to ask Jesus into your heart? Then ask him; it is that simple.*

- *Do you want out of the rat race many of us find ourselves in? Does your life have meaning and purpose the way it is being lived right now? Jesus will bring meaning to your life when you ask him to.*

- *Did you see how it is possible to go from a person totally trapped in the world's view of things, then be able to change into someone else?*

- *Did you see how you can know God and Jesus, think you are doing it right, and have it all wrong?*

- *Did you see and recognize the tools included in scripture and this book that help you know what to ask to get closer to the Lord and be empowered by him through his Spirit?*

- *Do you want to have so much of the Holy Spirit in you that he just bubbles out as a light of the world? Do you want to let God have control of your life now? Then ask him.*

- *Do you want to have the full resources of God literally at your fingertips? Do you truly desire for God to guide your every step? Would you really like to experience the power of God through the actions of the Holy Spirit? You can if you ask for it.*

- *Do you want to have peace in terrible circumstances and experience real joy of the Lord while still in those hard times? Then ask Him to come to you and go deeply into your heart and being!*

My prayer is you will be so moved by the Spirit of God, that your life will be transformed and renewed by His love through his Spirit. That you will become a new and powerful person and servant of God walking in the power of God for His glory! Amen.

—From Milk to Meat, Conclusion.